D0729004

The
Garden
of the
Soul

Cultivating Your Spiritual Life

Keri Wyatt Kent

Foreword by John Ortberg

InterVarsity Press

Downers Grove, Illinois

InterVarsity Press
P.O. Box 1400, Downers Grove, IL 60515-1426
World Wide Web: www.ivpress.com
E-mail: mail@ivpress.com

©2002 by Keri Wyatt Kent

All rights reserved. No part of this book may be reproduced in any form without written permission from InterVarsity Press.

InterVarsity Press® *is the book-publishing division of InterVarsity Christian Fellowship/USA*®, *a student movement active on campus at hundreds of universities, colleges and schools of nursing in the United States of America, and a member movement of the International Fellowship of Evangelical Students. For information about local and regional activities, write Public Relations Dept., InterVarsity Christian Fellowship/USA, 6400 Schroeder Rd., P.O. Box 7895, Madison, WI 53707-7895, or visit the IVCF website at <www.ivcf.org>.*

All Scripture quotations, unless otherwise indicated, are taken from the Holy Bible, New International Version®. NIV®. *Copyright ©1973, 1978, 1984 by International Bible Society. Used by permission of Zondervan Publishing House. All rights reserved.*

The song "I Will Worship You" was written by Joe Horness and Curt Coffield, copyright Ever Devoted Music, 2001. Used with permission.

Cover photograph: Tadashi Ono/Photonica

ISBN 0-8308-2349-2

Printed in the United States of America ∞

Library of Congress Cataloging-in-Publication Data

Kent, Keri Wyatt, 1963-

   The garden of the soul: cultivating your spiritual life / Keri Wyatt Kent.
     p. cm.
   Includes bibliographical references.
   ISBN 0-8308-2349-2 (paper: alk. paper)
     1. Gardening—Religious aspects—Christianity. 2. Spiritual life—Christianity. 3. Gardeners—Religious life. I. Title.

BV4596.G36 K46 2002
248.4—dc21

                                        2002023295

P	18	17	16	15	14	13	12	11	10	9	8	7	6	5	4	3	2	1
Y	16	15	14	13	12	11	10	09	08	07	06	05	04	03	02			

Contents

Foreword

There is no miracle like the miracle of growth. God's first command was to be fruitful. Humanity's first job was gardening. From the beginning of time growth has received our strongest efforts and greatest wonder.

And yet we wonder—when we're honest—can it really happen? I know it's supposed to, I know I can cultivate certain practices, but is it possible for a timid person to grow bold, for a bulldozer to gain a tender heart?

Keri joins an ancient stream of thinkers and writers who look at the growth of all living things and reflect on the growth of the heart. Jesus teaches the deep wisdom that we can't make it happen by ourselves, but we have much to do. The growth of the heart requires wisdom.

Keri writes as a mom, a wife and an active, real-world person. I remember hearing about a parent at a seminar on desert spirituality who asked—"Is there childcare in the desert?" If you ever ask that kind of question—"How is growth possible in *my* world?"—this book is for you. For it turns out that while there might not be childcare in the garden, caring for children can become one of the ways that God causes the garden of your soul to grow.

Keri's approach is accessible—anybody who really wants to grow can jump right in. It's also realistic—you don't have to resign from your life and go be a hermit someplace. Her voice will bring hope to people who may have felt stagnant for too long.

So here's to growth. Read the book—slowly if you can—but read it with an eye and ear for God's hand and voice.

John Ortberg

Acknowledgments

In the garden of my soul there are a few perennial relationships, ones that keep growing and blooming more profusely each year. Without them this book would never have been written.

Thank you to the leaders and body of Willow Creek Community Church, where I have served and learned and grown in community for fifteen years. Thanks especially to Ruth Haley Barton and John Ortberg, who have patiently led me to a way of being with God that is richer than I ever thought possible. Through godly example and encouraging words, you continue to teach me so much, and encourage and equip me to teach others. Each of you, in your own way, has challenged me to get out of the boat! Thanks so much.

I could not have survived the writing process without Bob Gordon, patient friend and ruthless editor. You helped me refine the writing and weather the storms of doubt. This project would have been impossible without your help. Thanks.

As I worked on this book, several friends who are much better gardeners than I welcomed me into their gardens and into their libraries. So thank you, Gina Young, Lynn Siewert and

Pam Howell for lending me your gardening books, and also for being women of integrity whose spiritual lives are even more beautiful than your backyard gardens. Your friendship nourishes my soul.

I also owe a debt of gratitude to my parents, who took my kids to the beach, the park, even mini-golfing while I sat in their basement and wrote several key chapters. Mom and Dad, you've blessed me with your encouragement and practical assistance over the years. Thank you.

Finally, thanks to Scot, Melanie and Aaron, who have patiently endured the writing process and all the things that go with it. You know quite well the weeds and rocks in the garden of my soul, but you love me anyway. I treasure you.

1

Winter

An Invitation
to a More Fruitful
Spiritual Life

When the ice of winter holds the house in its rigid grip,
when curtains are drawn early
against that vast frozen waste of landscape,
almost like a hibernating hedgehog
I relish the security of being withdrawn from that
summer ferment that is long since past.
Then is the time for reappraisal: to spread out,
limp and receptive, and let garden thoughts rise to the surface.
They emerge from some deep source of stillness
which the very fact of winter has released.

MIRABEL OSLER

*T*he quiet settles slowly, as if the whole house is catching its breath after the exuberant chaos of the morning.

A huge overnight storm had dumped nearly two feet of snow on us, and the kids were wild with excitement. The morning had been filled with countless trips out of the house to shovel the drive with their miniature red shovels and to build forts and snowmen and slides, each preceded by the requisite ten-minute wrestling match in which I bundled them into snowpants, boots, mittens and scarves. After fifteen minutes or so in the cold, the kids would troop back in for hot chocolate, dribbling off soggy layers of clothing in a sodden trail from door to kitchen as they came. I'd put the kettle on, throw their coats and snowpants into the dryer, find them dry socks. Soon, fortified with Swiss Miss and marshmallows, they'd be jumping up and down, saying, "Let's go out again! We have to finish our snow fort!"

But now, after lunch, I tiptoe around the house, amazed at the silence. My children and husband, exhausted from the morning's efforts, are sleeping all around the house.

My daughter, in her bed, surrounded by stuffed animals: a picture of peace in a three-dimensional frame.

My husband, on the couch in front of a muted football game.

My son, clutching his tattered blankie and lying on my husband's chest, his head tilted off of his daddy onto the couch at what looks like an awkward angle. But I don't dare try to move the statues. The way the two of them look together, and the silence, is too precious to risk disturbing.

So I retreat to the bedroom, a Diet Coke in hand. The pale winter sun, low in the sky even though it is early afternoon, comes through the ice-encrusted windows at an angle that shows all the dust on the dresser and bedside lamp. I ignore the dust, knowing I've fulfilled my admittedly low standards of domesticity by taking some time to throw a bit of leftover Christmas turkey, some rice and a can of mushroom soup into a casserole to serve for supper. Besides, I can dust when the kids are awake. Now I can be alone, guilt-free, for a little while (until the kids wake up).

I sit quietly for a moment, looking out the window, jotting a few notes in my journal, but mostly just sitting and listening to the quiet. I wait. I offer a quiet invitation to Jesus to join me here, in the unexpected silence, and then I wait again. I look out at the back yard, at the soft drifts that are now nearly as high as the back fence.

Where is God when I finally have a moment to meet with him? I know he's there, but at first I know it only on faith. And in that faith, whether I feel him or not, I take another step toward him and pick up my Bible.

I turn to John 15:1-4. "I am the true vine, and my Father is the gardener. . . . Remain in me, and I will remain in you. No branch can bear fruit by itself; it must remain in the vine. Neither can you bear fruit unless you remain in me."

Eugene Peterson translates another part of the same chapter: "Make yourselves at home in my love. If you keep my commands, you'll remain intimately at home in my love. That's what I've done—kept my Father's commands and made myself at home in his love" (John 15:9-10).*

What does it mean to bear fruit? How can I "remain intimately at home" in God's love? I've known these verses my whole life, but lately I find myself digging through them again and again. I've been a Christian, with varying degrees of commitment, for thirty years. But I don't think I've ever completely grasped what it means to "remain in Jesus," or as the King James Version says, "abide." I long for a fruitful life. I feel a sense of calling, of wanting to serve God, to have my life count for something in his kingdom. And it seems that the way to do that is to abide, to remain, to live in Jesus. But what does that mean? Just pray a lot? Think about God constantly? I'm not sure.

Once more I gaze out the window. I ask Jesus again to come. If I were really abiding in him, would I feel his presence more readily? I don't think so. Sometimes when I'm in this mode, this waiting for God, I think that actually he's waiting for me. He's waiting patiently for me to get still, to let go of my worries and my demands that he show up fast and soothe my hurried soul. Waiting for me to be quiet. I'm learning that you can't get really quiet on the inside in a hurry.

Slowly, eventually, the silence stops feeling so uncomfortable and begins to feed my soul. I imagine Jesus seated beside me in companionable quietness. Together we look out at the beauty of his handiwork, the snow spread like glittery frosting across the back yard. We don't say much.

Beneath the snow, whipped by sub-zero winds, lies my backyard garden. That, too, I know primarily on faith,

---

* The source of each quotation is listed in the notes section at the end of the book.

although some of the posts that support the chicken wire around its perimeter still stick through the two-foot drifts. But I am reminded of the garden by two other signs: the tomatoes, jams and pickles in canning jars that line the shelves of my kitchen cabinets (the fruit the garden produced last year), and the seed catalogs that arrived this week in the mail (inspiration for the future).

Ah, seed catalogs. Just paging through them, with their color photos of flowers and vegetables, brightens a gray winter afternoon. I dream of turning under the whole of our back yard to plant rows of everything from artichokes to zinnias. My husband complains that I've already claimed too much of the tiny yard and wonders if I can find another hobby that doesn't take up so much acreage. I remind him that he won't be complaining when I offer him summer lunches of BLTs made with home-grown tomatoes and lettuce. But he has a point: my good intentions and dreams of bountiful bouquets and sumptuous salads have often prompted me to order more seeds than I need. My garden plans often far exceed my gardening realities.

Looking at seed catalogs is a bit like reading the Bible for me. Not because I am so zealous a gardener, but because it inspires me to want to produce fruit—in the case of seed catalogs, fruit of an edible kind, and with the Bible, fruit of a spiritual kind.

A Growing Obsession

I have not always been a gardener. But over the past ten years or so my interest and expertise in gardening have been, shall we say, growing.

It began when my husband and I moved from our little condo to a house with a yard. The previous owners had planted a few perennials, most notably a gorgeous climbing rose on the side of the house and a single peony bush in the back yard. That first spring in our new house the roses bloomed profusely, as did the peony at the same time. I picked both and arranged the deep red and pale pink flowers in a crystal bowl. The result surprised and delighted me so much, I took a picture of the arrangement.

From there I started checking out gardening books from the library and inviting friends who were far more experienced gardeners over to help me figure out what to plant and how to make it flourish, how to expand the flower beds and divide the hostas.

Eventually I got into vegetable gardening and actually took a class to learn how to put food up by canning and freezing it. My hobby became a way to provide food for our family and gifts for friends.

Although gardening required some work on my part, I loved seeing (and eating) the results of my efforts. I found deep pleasure just walking through the back yard and seeing things blooming or ripening. I must admit, my first efforts at gardening were rather disorganized, with plants thrown everywhere without much of a plan. I'd see something on sale at the garden center, bring it home and tuck it in somewhere. Lately I've been learning about the importance, both agriculturally and aesthetically, of a well-ordered garden.

Today I can't imagine my life without my garden. It brings me countless small joys: the way my front yard looks in the spring, the taste of fresh asparagus or tomatoes, the smell of a bouquet of flowers. Whether I'm able to spend a lot of time or a little gardening, it will always be a part of who I am.

My Soul's Garden

Just as my interest in flowers and vegetables has grown, so has my desire to better understand how it is that human beings grow spiritually. What makes one person grow, while another seems to whither, or just fail to thrive? How can I grow? Lately I've been reading books and consulting experts on just what makes the garden of the soul flourish.

So often the fruit I want and the fruit I actually produce are very different. In the garden the chipmunks or slugs attack my tomatoes. Or I plant seeds but don't give them enough water or fertilizer to make them produce more than a few blooms.

Likewise, my spiritual life rarely lives up to my intentions. I want to abide, and I want to see the spiritual fruit like joy and peace and patience. I want to be like a tree planted by streams of water. But I get distracted, I get busy. I'm uncertain about how to remain in Jesus. And sometimes it feels like winter in the garden of my soul: no fruit, no flowers. Just sticks and chicken wire protruding through the snow.

In winter the garden is a sketch in a notebook, a vision in my head. It is a season of planning and preparing, of dreaming about what I will plant and ordering the seeds or plants to make it happen. Mostly it is a season of waiting. While I draw up garden plans, the snow feeds the soil and allows it the rest it needs to be productive.

As cold and uncomfortable as winter sometimes feels, it is a necessary season. And though it seems no fruit is borne, the Master Gardener is working, sketching out the plans of what he's going to grow in the garden of my soul. Jeremiah 29:11 tells of God's grace to his people, his desires for us: "'For I know the plans I have for you,' declares the Lord, 'plans to prosper you and not to harm you, plans to give you a hope and a future.'" That's his promise, even when we are feeling as though we are exiled or distant from God.

As I sit quietly gazing at the snow, I wonder what fruit the coming year will bring. Jesus said that his followers would be known by the fruit in their lives. When we are living the life of the Spirit, the result, the Bible promises, will be evident in our lives: like trees planted by streams of water, like branches of a vine, we will bear fruit.

What does that mean to us in a world where it seems as if grapes grow in the produce section of the Super Kmart? Galatians 5:22-23 provides us a list of the attributes that the fruit has: "The fruit of the Spirit is love, joy, peace, patience, kindness, goodness, faithfulness, gentleness and self-control." Notice that Paul writes the *fruit*, not the *fruits*. There are not seven different fruits, but seven attributes, or characteristics, of spiritual fruit.

When we have the Holy Spirit in our lives, we will begin to produce this fruit. This list is not a list of "shoulds" or "ought to's" for followers of Christ. It is a description of what God is like, and what, if we let him, he will cultivate in the garden of our souls. The passage paints a picture of what God's children are becoming—that is, more like what God already is.

The trouble is, I'm sometimes not very loving, and I lose my patience a lot. I have moments of joy, but sometimes I'm just angry or complaining. So does that mean I'm not "walking in the Spirit"? Am I a failure as a Christian?

I cannot, by sheer willpower, by reading self-help books or

even praying "really hard," make myself more loving, more patient or more gentle. But if I rightly understand what each of these attributes looks like, I can cultivate them. How? Through spiritual disciplines, or practices, that will enable me over time to do what I can't do by simply "trying harder."

Spiritual practices, such as solitude, self-examination or reflective reading, strengthen my connection with Jesus. They help me provide the optimum growing environment for my soul. They are a part of my spiritual process, but *not* the end result.

If someone asks me how my garden is doing, I don't say: "Well, I've been weeding it daily and giving it plenty of water, and I spent quite a bit of time working some manure into the vegetable patch last week."

Instead I eagerly reply, "Oh, you should see the tomatoes we've got this year, and my roses looked absolutely breathtaking last month. I've already made five batches of pesto from the basil plants—they're huge. Do you need any zucchini? I've got a little extra."

But if someone were to ask me how my spiritual life is going, I don't talk about the fruit. I talk about the weeding and the manure. "Well, I've been trying to have a consistent quiet time, and I've been doing a lot of Bible study." I point to the cultivation methods, mistaking them for fruit.

When I read a passage like the one in Galatians about spiritual fruit, I fall into seed catalog mode and I think: That's what I want my life to look like: love, joy, peace, patience. I'd like to order several packets of each. But like the pests that undermine my vegetable gardening efforts, the distractions and busyness of my life (that is, my kids, my schedule, my work) attack my efforts to be a fruitful Christian. Or so I think.

It's easy to misinterpret the list of attributes in Galatians 5 as a sort of religious to-do list, a sort of measuring stick that we judge ourselves with: "Well, I'm pretty loving, but I need some work on the patience thing." (Which is rather self-delusional, since the Bible says, "Love is patient." I mean, if that's true, how can I be truly loving but not patient?)

And have you ever tried to become more patient just by gritting your teeth and trying really hard? I have. I'll decide to be a model mother and that I will just be patient with my children all day. Despite the fact that I really do love my children and want very much to be patient, my effort typically lasts until about breakfast and the first spill or the second tantrum or . . . you get the idea. Attempts to force myself to be fruitful often result in plastic fruit.

But Paul is describing the *fruit* of the Spirit, not the *fruits*. He's describing what someone who has the Spirit in their life is like. Just as an apple (which starts out small, hard, sour and green) matures into a fruit that is red, crunchy, sweet, white on the inside and round, a disciple of Christ will mature into someone who is increasingly loving, kind, gentle, good and self-controlled. Christians cannot become all these things by direct effort. Paul's point is that those who have the Spirit guiding them will grow in all of these things as a result of the Spirit's influence and guidance. He's not giving a list for us to try and achieve on our own, or worse yet, pick and choose from. We can't say, "Well, I'll work on being kind, but I can't manage that gentleness thing."

What good is an apple that's red and crunchy but tastes sour? Or one that is round and red outside but brown and rotten inside? Fruit doesn't get credit for being "pretty good." And it can't improve its condition by trying harder. It gets thrown out.

God created apples in the first place, along with rain and sun and soil and everything else that makes them grow. The apples themselves don't have a lot to say in the matter. The ones that "succeed" as apples are the ones that manage to stay on the tree until harvest time. (There's that abiding thing again!)

I cannot create an apple, but I can provide optimum conditions to help it grow. I know if I do not protect it from pests or give it enough water, it is likely to lose the attribute of crispness. If I give it too little or too much water at certain times, the fruit may not ripen properly. The way I fertilize and water and cultivate the soil around an apple tree will determine the extent to which it conforms to the ideal for apples: red, crisp, sweet, tart.

Similarly certain spiritual practices will cultivate, over time, the fruit of the Spirit in my life. Since the fruit is "of the Spirit," the Spirit obviously plays a key role in my transformation. In other words, my activities alone won't make me more patient or loving. That's what Jesus was talking about in John 15. A branch can't bear fruit by itself. But spiritual practices, if we approach them as ways to strengthen our ability to remain in Christ, provide the optimum growing conditions for God to do his work.

The apostle Paul knew that God is the one who ultimately causes growth. When some of his newer converts were trying to give him credit for their growth and arguing with others who

thought another teacher, Apollos, was better, Paul set the record straight: "I planted the seed, Apollos watered it, but God made it grow. So neither he who plants nor he who waters is anything, but only God, who makes things grow" (1 Corinthians 3:6-7).

Whether you think someone else can

make you grow by leading or teaching you, or you think you alone are responsible for your growth, you can learn from Paul's admonition. You are not your pastor's garden, or your spouse's, but God's. As the Living Bible translates verse 9 in this chapter, "We are only God's co-workers. You are *God's* garden, not ours; you are *God's* building, not ours."

Pruning and Protection

A cherry tree grows in our back yard. It was here when we moved in. For the first few years we lived in this house, we didn't even harvest the cherries. We never pruned the tree (we claim ignorance), so it only produced a sparse crop, which was gobbled up by the birds.

One year a friend who was a bit more experienced in this type of thing told us to prune the tree right after it had borne its fruit. So when the birds finished their banquet, my husband pulled out the ladder and the hack saw and trimmed away, quite severely, I thought. The next spring we bought some plastic netting, and after a number of comical attempts (which involved a five-pound weight tied to the net and a few dings in the aluminum siding), we managed to toss the net over the tree. It had grown considerably despite (actually, because of) the pruning. The net foiled the birds' attempts to snack on the cherries. The result: fruit. A lot of fruit.

We were amazed to see how many cherries that little tree was capable of producing. We had cherry pies, cherry preserves, cherry cobbler, cherries in abundance. It is one thing to read about fruit and vines and branches. It is another to live with the reality of peanut butter and cherry jam sandwiches through a long Midwestern winter.

Like the cherry tree, our lives are sometimes more fruitful

after we've been pruned and protected. As I allow the Master Gardener access to my life, he may notice that I have a few branches that need pruning. It may feel painful, even severe, at the time. But fruit will result.

Just as my cherry tree couldn't produce any cherries by its own efforts, neither can I produce goodness or gentleness, for example, by merely trying hard. The fruit of the Spirit is a gift. It is the outward evidence of my inward relationship with Jesus. I can't work to produce it. But I can take steps to make sure the garden of my soul has optimum growing conditions, and sometimes those ideal conditions are created not by what we give, but by what we take away.

If I want to see fruit in my life, I may have to be obedient to God's boundaries. Like the net on the tree, God's laws protect me. And I have to be a good steward of my time and energy, setting boundaries so that my soul is not depleted by hungry birds who just want my time and energy. Too many obligations, even noble ones, will ravage the garden of my soul.

Planning for a Fruitful Harvest

My most fruitful gardening seasons come as a result of having a plan. Dedicated gardeners spend the winter poring over seed catalogs and then sketching plans that show what they will plant in each part of the garden. They read books to get ideas about how to make a garden beautiful and productive, about what to plant and when to plant it. When I plant haphazardly or order seeds without making a plan, my garden is not as beautiful and not as fruitful. In my first few years as a gardener, I had a rather disorganized garden. But as it developed, I saw the value in planning my plantings.

There's also great value in planning our spiritual gardens.

John Ortberg writes, "Spiritual transformation cannot be orchestrated or controlled, but neither is it a random venture. We need some kind of support or structure, much as a young vine needs a trellis."

When I was first introduced to the idea of having a spiritual plan, I balked. I'm not sure why. Usually I like to plan. I am not really a play-it-by-ear sort of person. If I'm willing to sketch out a garden plan, why does it feel so uncomfortable to make a spiritual plan?

Planning to grow spiritually seemed to take the mystery out of it. I was afraid I would take over and plan God right out of the equation. What role would God play if I were making plans? Isn't spiritual growth sort of a mystical thing?

Yes, indeed it is. Yet the mystery is this: God cares enough to speak to me, to direct me in making a plan for cultivating the garden of my soul. I can't make myself grow any more than I can make the flowers in my garden grow. I can't even come up with a workable plan without God's help. But with his guidance I can make some progress. Any plan, whether for a garden or for a spiritual life, has to include cooperation with God.

I cannot plan where the growth will take me. But I can plan to incorporate certain disciplines into my life. Which ones? The ones that God shows me and tells me that I need, or draws me to by creating a desire for them in my heart. My plans begin with listening to God, hearing what it is he'd have me do, or not do, and then obeying. If I cooperate with God in this way, I can expect to see spiritual fruit as a result.

Every Little Thing Matters

You may think of spiritual disciplines only as the peculiar practices of monks or gurus, like meditation and fasting. But other less traditional disciplines can encourage the fruit of the Spirit to grow in my life. I for one have seen firsthand that love and patience and gentleness have no better place to grow than in Candy Land.

You may not think that playing Candy Land is a spiritual discipline, but let me assure you, if you are the parent of preschoolers, it most certainly is. Even if you stack the deck so your daughter gets Queen Frostine and you get Plumpy, so that she wins and wins quickly (don't pretend you haven't done this, moms), playing a game with your child is a way of demonstrating long-suffering patience and love.

Jesus said there's no greater love than this: that you lay down your life for a friend. As a mom, I would lay down my life for my kids, fight to the death to defend them. My life, sure. My agenda? That's another story. But if I play a game with my kids when I don't really feel like it (and when do I ever really feel like it?), I'm cultivating love by laying down my agenda.

I can't abandon my agenda 100 percent of the time. Sometimes I have to do things that require at least part of my attention. Things like clearing a path through the toys to the door so that we can get out of the house. Or getting the load of white clothes into the dryer so that everyone will have clean underwear. Or meeting the deadline on a magazine article.

Yet, love does not demand its own way. Sometimes, in order to love my kids, I need to give up what I want to do and just spend time listening to them, reading with them, just hanging out with them. It doesn't always feel important because there's often no task that we accomplish. Work, errands, household chores, phone calls and other projects can easily cut into time that I could spend with my kids.

If I can put aside my concerns and live fully in the present moment, my spirit becomes more loving, more patient, more gentle. Because it's not about the game, it's about the opportunity to demonstrate to your kids what unselfish love looks like. They probably won't appreciate how much of a sacrifice it is right now, but that's okay. Even if they never appreciate it, you will be formed by it.

If I think about living intentionally, paying attention to where I am and where my kids are right now, I can lay down my life for a while. I can love.

For my kids, love is expressed through play. Through them I am learning that God's love, though it is rich and deep and even mysterious, can also be playful. It's hard for me to love in a rich, deep or mysterious way. But playful I can learn to do. It may not seem that big of a deal or feel very spiritual to me, but God can use it to develop spiritual fruit. Every little thing you do can have God in it, if you invite him to be with you.

Working Together with God

I can till the soil in my garden, digging and hoeing and removing rocks and weeds. I can plant tomato seeds and fertilize them. I can water them regularly, stake the plants and put cages around them to keep them from flopping over. I can prune off unproductive branches and remove wilted leaves. I can gingerly pluck off the slugs, if necessary. That's my part. But I can't tell you the exact number of tomatoes I'll harvest or what day they'll begin to turn red. I can't sit out in the garden and force the tomatoes to grow or ripen. That part is up to God and the whim of the weather, which he ultimately controls.

Likewise, I can plant seeds of truth by reading or listening to teaching on spiritual truth. I can spend time praying, listening to worship tapes or just sitting in silence. I can plan for times of solitude, where I can be alone with God, and set boundaries that protect that time. I can prune my busy schedule so that I have time for what really matters, like playing board games with my kids.

But I cannot make myself grow. I do not know when God will produce a harvest, when he will feed others through my words or actions. Together God and I till the soil of my soul and prepare it for fruitfulness.

Sometimes in a garden there are big jobs, like transplanting or digging new beds. But mostly, effective gardening is about maintenance, about pulling the weeds and watering and dead-heading the flowers. You could do some of these tasks once a week, but I've found that if you pull weeds and water the garden each day, not only does the garden flourish, but the tending of it is more enjoyable and less tiresome.

The heart of gardening is the little daily interactions with the plants and the soil. Likewise, the heart of spiritual growth is in every little thing you do throughout your day. If I experience solitude only when my kids and husband happen to fall asleep on a snowy Saturday afternoon, the benefits will not be as great as if I make solitude and other practices a regular part of my routine.

I long for fruit in my spiritual life: feeling joyful and close to God, being able to share his love and truth with friends, being gentle and self-controlled in my words and actions, being loving and patient with my children. But I don't want to be pruned, because it might hurt. Often I resist the limits God sets to protect me, since a net over me feels too restrictive. I don't want to make time for practices that will improve the growing conditions in the garden of my soul.

So how can I live in such a way that the fruit of the Spirit grows in my life? That's what I am trying to learn about. I am trying to open my soul to God in small ways each day, so that he can come in and do the work that will help me grow and flourish. I invite you to come with me as I learn to cultivate the garden of my soul.

Digging deeper

These questions will help you get the most out of this book. Use them for personal reflection, perhaps journaling your answers. Or read the book with a group of people and use the questions to guide your discussion.

1. Describe a time when you felt intimately connected to God. What do you think helped you to be able to "abide in Christ" in that season of your life?

2. When you look at Paul's description of the fruit of the Spirit in Galatians 5:22-23 and look at your own spiritual life, do you see any similarities? Which of these characteristics do you feel God is calling you to cultivate? Which seems most challenging?

3. Describe the current state of the garden of your soul. What season is it? What's growing there: weeds, potatoes, roses? How is the condition of the soil? Draw a picture or write a paragraph about your garden.

2

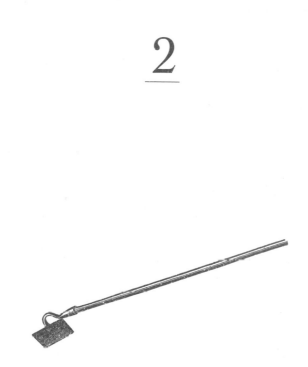

Soil

Submitting Yourself
to God's Cultivating Work

*The Christian knows that while
tending the garden there are no easy strolls with God.
It is not that gardening is valueless
or purposeless or wants of reward.
But the fruit of sweet communion comes
after the gall and the vinegar.*
VIGEN GUROIAN

*A*s winter begins to melt away, I get rather anxious to get out in the garden. While we may get occasional warm days in early spring, unfortunately I can't start gardening right away.

Before planting in the spring, any gardener will tell you that you must "work" the soil. Basically this means digging it up, adding fertilizer as needed, preparing it for planting. You need to clear it of weeds and rocks and chop up any hard clumps of earth so that seeds will have a chance to grow. It requires a bit of sweat and effort, but mostly it just takes some time.

Planting instructions for some early plants say the seeds can be sown in spring, "as soon as the soil can be worked." Frozen soil, or soil so saturated that it is simply mud, is not ready for planting. Some seeds can't be planted until the soil has warmed. Any effort will be in vain if it is not done at the proper time.

Before a season of growth, in his perfect timing, God has often put his shovel into the soil of my soul. He digs things up, breaks apart the hard clumps. This is absolutely no fun at all. It's painful, but necessary, if growth is to result. Sometimes he'll find just mud and know that what I need is time.

Early spring gardening is hard work and little else. Except for the occasional snowdrops or crocuses peeking through the snow and ice, there are few blooms and no fruit. Not yet.

Some seasons are for waiting and working.

Our most productive seasons come when we work patiently with God in this cultivating process, when we invest time in waiting, then time in working. Look at Luke 13, where Jesus tells a short parable about an unproductive fig tree. Though the tree's owner wanted it cut down, the gardener convinced him to wait. "Leave it alone for one more year, and I'll dig around it and fertilize it. If it bears fruit next year, fine! If not, then cut it down" (Luke 13:8-9).

When we get impatient with not seeing spiritual fruit in our lives, God tells us to wait and to let him do some digging. Henry Cloud comments on this parable: "Using the trowel of God's truth, we must dig out the weeds and encumbrances of falsehood, sin and hurt that keep the soil of our souls cluttered. In addition, we must add the fertilizer of love and relationship to 'enrich the soil.'"

How is it that God digs out the weeds and rocks in the soil of our soul? With his truth. Sometimes he reveals that truth through leadings or gentle whispers. His Spirit may convict us of unhealthy patterns, be they in relationships, in activities, in the way we take care of ourselves.

At other times God uses the truth of Scripture, or the truth-telling of a friend, to dig around in our souls. My spiritual life will be unfruitful unless I allow that digging, even arrange for it to happen. Sometimes that means asking a friend to have a look around.

Identifying Weeds

When spring comes, I am always amazed by my perennial garden, where the plants that appeared to be dead resurrect themselves to bloom, even bigger than last year. But early in spring, before things flower, I often have trouble telling the weeds from the flowers. I'm tempted to let the weeds just grow, to see if they are actually daisies.

When my friend Gina eyes the perennial bed, she points to a particularly hardy specimen and asks, "What's that?"

"I'm not sure," I admit. "But last year I had the same thing, and I think it bloomed very nicely at the end of June."

"It's a weed," this experienced gardener informs me. "Pull it."

I invite Gina into my garden because she is honest with me about what's growing there. She doesn't tell me what she thinks I'd like to hear. Sometimes she shatters my illusions. I don't always want to receive her advice, but upon reflection I know she is right. She tells me the truth about what's a weed and what's a flower, what's working and what needs some changing. And she sometimes brings something from her garden to share, like columbine or maybe some seeds she's saved. My garden is healthier because of her influence.

One way to find the weeds in the garden of your soul is to invite others to have a look around. God often uses other people to cultivate, to speak truth. Seek out people you consider to be spiritually wise or discerning to help you distinguish the weeds from the flowers, to be truth-tellers for you. Do you have people in your life who are experts, or at least more expert than you are, when it comes to spiritual matters? Would they be willing to guide you or offer their advice?

If you have such a person in your life, you are blessed. But it will still take courage to invite them in and listen to what they have to say, receiving and acting upon it. And if someone is willing to take the time to point out the weeds in the garden of your soul, you have to be willing to pull them.

Even "good" plants, like mint, can eventually take over a garden. Mint is what gardening books refer to as an invasive plant, meaning that it can spread throughout a garden if it is not contained. Each week in summer I have to pull up armloads of mint by its roots because it has sprung up among the tomatoes and zucchini. If I leave it there, it will choke out the other plants.

What are the weeds in the garden of your soul? In mine, the biggest thistle bush is busyness. Doing too much. I chop it down, but it seems to sprout up again quickly. If I am busy, especially with family or church activities, I sometimes mistake it for something good, like a flower. But hurry and busyness do not produce spiritual fruit, or beauty. They choke out what God is trying to create in my soul. I need to pull the weeds of busyness and hurry from the garden of my soul so that the flowers have room to bloom.

And of course, as soon as I pull one weed, others pop up — like worry, especially worrying about what other people think of me. The weed of impression management has deep roots in my garden. Maybe for you, weeds of fear or addictive behavior or gossip or pride are choking out your efforts to grow.

Even good things, like work or ministry or even caring for my children, can become invasive, like mint. What good plants in the garden of your soul are taking over, choking out the more tender things like time with God or time for yourself?

Working the Soil

Before planting, serious gardeners often run a soil test. They gather a small amount of soil from their garden and send it off to a lab or run it through an at-home test. The test provides information on the pH level of the soil, so that they know what nutrients to add to optimize growth of whatever they want to plant.

Hydrangeas, for example, love acidic soil. So if your soil is too alkaline, hydrangeas won't grow. In fact, I take my coffee grounds out each morning and dump them next to the hydrangea, just to give it a good boost of acidic material.

But the pH level of the soil is only one small factor. If the soil is full of rocks or so hard-packed you can't break through it with a shovel or if it's full of weeds, the acidity or alkalinity doesn't matter. In the garden, soil must be worked, the rocks and weeds removed, before anything can grow there.

Likewise, we need to examine the soil of our souls before we can expect anything to grow there. If it's choked with weeds (like busyness or fear), full of rocks (like anger or addiction) or depleted of nutrients (because of burnout or exhaustion), we'll be frustrated in our efforts to grow.

Matthew 13 records Jesus' parable about a farmer who sowed seed on different kinds of soil: hard-packed soil; rocky, shallow soil; soil choked with thorny weeds; and finally, good soil. Jesus explains later in the chapter what the various types of soil represent.

Notice the good soil. "But what was sown on good soil is the man who hears the word and understands it. He produces a crop, yielding a hundred, sixty or thirty times what was sown" (Matthew 13:23).

In other words, hearing and understanding God's Word will result in fruitfulness in my life. But I need to have good soil. And good soil is soil that has been worked, making it friable and soft. Sometimes that means God has to get out the shovel and turn things over, dig things up.

Working the soil can also involve mixing in compost or fertilizer

to the soil before we plant. These simple chores loosen and improve the soil, making it easier for things to grow. Flowers bloom more vigorously. Vegetable plants become more prolific.

When God is working the soil of your soul, sometimes it feels like he is churning things up, mixing in some manure-like things, like suffering or difficulties, to make the soil stronger, better able to produce fruit.

Several years ago my husband was laid off right before our second child was born. I felt like everything was getting turned upside down and broken apart. I was depressed, although I tried very hard to pretend that everything was okay. Sometimes I cried out to God, other times I just cried. I couldn't see it at the time, but God was working the soil of my soul. Eventually that painful season produced spiritual fruit in my life. I was gentler, I believe, and also had begun to learn what it really meant to trust God.

About a year or so later things seemed to be getting better. Then God apparently decided to dig a little deeper, to break apart some additional clumps in the soil of my soul.

My best friend had helped me get through the struggles of that wintery year. Both of us felt like the other was the close friend we had hoped and prayed to find. We were soul mates, and our children were best friends. We talked on the phone often; we got together almost every week.

Then she told me the news: she and her family were moving. To Florida. Within the year.

I was sad. I was angry. I had prayed for a close friend, some-one who understood me and loved me, someone that I could be real with. Robin had been the answer to that prayer, I thought. So why was God taking her away from me?

Looking back, I can see that my friendship with Robin was a

treasure, but it was one that I was holding too tightly. God wanted to be first in my life, and I can't honestly say that he always was. So God did a little work in the soil of my soul. He took the spade and broke apart the hard clumps in my heart. He gave me a rainy season. Things looked gray and dismal, but that time prepared me for a season of growth.

What's amazing is that although this long-distance friendship has had its share of difficulties, we are still close. We can still be brutally honest with each other. And our relationship is healthier, I think, because I can't always turn to her for my day-to-day emotional needs. I have to ask God for those, and he uses a variety of other friends to meet many of those needs. It has strengthened my dependence on Christ and put human relationships, which are indeed precious, in proper perspective.

How Does Your Garden Grow?
Even if we are gardening diligently, being very intentional, our garden is not going to spring into full bloom overnight. Be gentle with yourself, and patient. Despite how slow growth may seem, it does happen, if you make sure the conditions are right.

In my garden the plants will grow—if I provide nutrients in the soil, plenty of water, protection from pests and a sunny location. It may not grow in ways I expect, and I can't control every outcome. Ultimately the timing and extent of the growth is up to God. Still, the chances for a flourishing garden are much greater when I provide optimal conditions.

Spiritual disciplines are tools that help us to cultivate the garden of our souls. Combined with the work of God in our lives, they help us create a healthy environment for growth.

The disciplines are spiritual practices or exercises that strengthen our souls, just as physical training strengthens our bodies. When I first started going to an aerobics class a few years ago, I could not keep up. I would stop, trying to catch my breath. I would grapevine left when I was supposed to go right. I would literally trip over my own feet. But as I continued to engage in the discipline of showing up for aerobics class, I found that I learned the moves and my fitness level increased. My body got stronger through physical training. Over time I was able to do what I couldn't do before. That's the result of physical training.

Spiritual disciplines are simply spiritual training tools. They will, over time, help me develop the conditions in the garden of my soul that will strengthen my connection to God. They will help me bear fruit, with the help of God, that I could not produce by simply trying to do so.

"Spiritual disciplines are like garden tools. The best spade and hoe in the world cannot guarantee a good crop. They only make it more likely that growth will be unobstructed," writes Marjorie Thompson in *Soul Feast*. "The mystery of maturation lies in the heart of the seed, and the outcome of planting depends largely on the vagaries of the weather. Still, tools are important in helping to ensure that planted seeds will bear fruit."

An Impossible Dream?

I can hear you grumbling now, especially if you have young children. "I barely have time for a shower in the mornings. I'd love just to go to the bathroom by myself, and you're telling me about meditation and solitude?"

It is precisely because we think that we do not have a minute to ourselves that we need to carve out time to be alone, to focus on our own growth rather than someone else's.

This book is not intended to make anyone feel guilty. As I

write, my daughter comes into the room and begins jumping on my bed and talking to me, despite the fact that I asked my husband to watch the kids for an hour this morning while I try to write. A moment later my son wanders in, making little puppy-like noises and trying to climb onto my lap. My husband is fixing breakfast, and I shoo them downstairs.

I do not have a formal quiet time every day. But I do make time for some time alone, even if it's just five minutes. I try to get to it first thing in the morning, but it sometimes doesn't happen until just before I go to bed at night. I may not always follow a formula for prayer, but I do take a few moments of silence. Long periods of solitude are rare (for that matter, even short ones happen infrequently), and I have to fight tooth and nail for any time to focus on my own spiritual (or even physical) needs. But the key to cultivating the garden of my soul is to live intentionally: to be aware of God's constant presence around me, to be aware of God's efforts to teach and connect with me, even in the seemingly chaotic moments of my day. How can I cultivate such awareness? It begins when I take even five minutes to be absolutely still and quiet.

A friend of mine who has four kids ranging in age from three to fifteen carries her Bible with her in the car. "You never know when you might get a few minutes for a quiet time," she says. I know what she's talking about. I've sat in my car in the parking lot at the mall, journaling my prayers while both kids slept in the back seat.

But my friend with the Bible in her car also recently left her children with her husband for two days, checked into a bed and breakfast an hour or so away from home and enjoyed a weekend of solitude and spiritual reflection. She's both realistic and intentional, and the garden of her soul is thriving as a result.

I have to keep reminding myself that I don't earn extra points for doing more disciplines, more spiritual activities. Spiritual disciplines are not a way to impress God, but a way of strengthening our connection with him, especially in areas where we are weak. What's important is to listen to God and obey his direction, to submit to his cultivating efforts.

Everything that happens to you has God in it. All you need to do is cultivate your ability to see it. This is no small task, but it is possible. When we decide we want to be intentional about growth and take practical steps to make the soil of our souls more fertile, the God who longs to connect with us does amazing things.

When I fail or fall short, I try not to beat myself up. I accept God's grace for the season I'm in, but I don't stop my attempts to cultivate the garden of my soul. I do what I can do and engage in the practices I know I need, knowing that if I keep it up, I'll be able to do what I could not before. Where once grew only weeds, flowers begin to bloom.

Take a Good Look Around

If I want to cultivate the garden of my soul, I've got to get out in the garden and take a look at what's growing there: the good, the bad and the ugly. I can do this by engaging in what the founders of Alcoholics Anonymous called "a fearless and searching moral inventory." In other words, I need to practice the discipline of self-examination.

This inventory is not something you can do in a few minutes. It is likely to be an ongoing process that takes several weeks or more. However, I think it is helpful to begin by setting aside a few hours of solitude to do what is known as a "life review." In such an exercise you might journal about various fears and feelings, and try to understand first your shortcomings and then your strengths. Reflect on questions like, What are my strengths? What are my weaknesses? What tempts me? What am I afraid of? Do I say I believe one thing but act as if I believe something else entirely?

Once you have completed this inventory, you can use it to guide you through review of the day or "the daily examen." Unlike a more complete moral inventory, daily self-examination means simply taking a few minutes to appraise your actions and attitudes. Did we give in to the weaknesses we uncovered in our more thorough self-examination? On a daily basis we should take a few minutes to ask ourselves some fearless and searching questions, such as: What exactly was I trying to prove by bragging about my accomplishments when I spoke to my neighbor yesterday? Where did I see God in my day? Did I notice him at all? Is there envy, anger, sadness in my heart? Where is that coming from? Are there unconfessed sins or grudges that are putting a barrier between God and me? Between others and me? Do I cope with life's stresses in unhealthy ways? Are there patterns developing? What is the next step that God wants me to take in my life? Am I willing to take it?

This is not an invitation to beat yourself up or become mired in guilt. It's just a chance to acknowledge the truth about yourself, the truth that God already knows and loves you in spite of. As we see what's growing (or not growing) in the garden of our souls, we know which tools we need to use to improve things.

"While the truth that we cannot escape God's all-seeing eye may weigh us down at times, it is finally the only remedy for our uneasiness," Thompson writes in *Soul Feast*. "When we feel 'searched and known' by a gracious God, we are both moved and enabled to search our own hearts honestly."

We can use the fruit of the Spirit as a paradigm for self-examination. Am I becoming more loving than I was a year ago? Am I more peaceful? How often do I lose my patience—more frequently or less frequently than a month ago, for instance?

Another tool for self-examination is to read through the Ten Commandments (Exodus 20:1-17), or Paul's description of Christian love in 1 Corinthians 13:4-7. Ask yourself, *How am I doing in each of these areas? Am I patient? Am I kind? Do I hold grudges?*

Obviously we can't ask ourselves these types of questions while we're doing the laundry. They require us to move into solitude, if even for an hour or two, and really listen to what God is trying to tell us.

That takes courage, at least for me. It is scary to pray the words of Psalm 139:23-24: "Search me, O God, and know my heart; test me and know my anxious thoughts. See if there is any offensive way in me, and lead me in the way everlasting."

God does search our hearts, and he does know us. And that is both comforting and unnerving. God really does know me and loves me anyway. And he'll lead me. Armed with this truth, I can venture into the garden and examine it. I can find the weeds or rocks that are keeping the fruit of the Spirit from growing in my life.

Once we figure out our weaknesses, we'll know which tools to use to improve things. We'll choose to engage in certain disciplines to get stronger in areas where we are currently weak.

"People who think that they are spiritually superior because they make a practice of a discipline such as fasting or silence or frugality are entirely missing the point," writes Dallas Willard. "The need for extensive practice of a given discipline is an indication of our weakness, not our strength. We can even lay it down as a rule of thumb that if it is easy for us to engage in a certain discipline, we probably don't need to practice it."

Telling the Truth

Once we have figured out what trips us up, it's good to have a conversation with God about it. This is not easy for me. I tend to beat around the bush a bit when I have to confess something: "You know, Lord . . . well, of course you *know*, you're omnipotent, after all, but anyway, what I need to tell you is, I'm struggling just a wee bit with the pride thing. What other people think of me is getting a little too important. So I feel pretty spiritual for having figured this out, which of course lands me right back in the pride patch again. So, Lord, as you can see, I need a little help with this. Starting with forgiveness, if you wouldn't mind. And a little help on staying humble. Of course, not too much help because if you humble me too much it could be embarrassing." And so it goes.

God is likely listening to my ramblings, slightly amused. But when I finally get to the point and name my sin, I can pray, "Lord, have mercy on me, a sinner." And despite my messy confession, God's mercy rains down on the soil of my soul.

Confessing to God should be a daily discipline, one we include every time we spend time in prayer, and one that a pang of conviction prompts in us as an immediate response. Until we know the pain of confession, we can't experience the joy of forgiveness.

In order to really examine our souls, to listen to what God is telling us, to be able to bask in his love and forgiveness, we are going to have to get quiet. We are going to need to go to the garden alone. Transformation begins to happen when I set boundaries in my life that create some sacred space, when I enter into solitude and find God there.

 **Digging deeper**

1. What weeds tend to crop up in the garden of your soul? Do you have someone in your life—a friend, a spouse, a mentor—who can help you to see the weeds? If not, what steps could you take (joining a small group, for example) to find one? How do you feel (fear? excitement? uncertainty?) about allowing someone that kind of access to your life?

2. Where has God been working the soil in your life lately? What parts of your life are hard-packed or rocky?

3. How does it feel to be alone, with unconfessed sin in your heart? What are you alone with right now? What steps could you take to change that?

3

Fence

Meeting God
in Solitude and Silence

God could have put us on a beach,
on a mountain, in a desert or in the ocean.
But he chose to plant a garden especially for us.
God is the original Gardener.
Those of us who know the joys of a garden have a deep
understanding of where we are meant to be.
By bare-handedly working the earth and tending its fruits,
we better know the Creator.

LOIS TRIGG CHAPLIN

*M*y backyard garden is really several small islands in a sea of lawn. An archipelago made up of several vegetable islands, a perennial peninsula, a cluster of containers on the deck.

Each bed has some manner of fence at its perimeter. Some are made of chicken wire and wooden stakes, others, just a row of bricks a few inches high. The fencing provides boundaries for the vegetable plots, keeping at least some little pests at bay. Rabbits in search of a nibble of lettuce are foiled by the chicken wire. The brick edging shows me where the flowerbed ends and the lawn begins, so that when I'm mowing, I don't cut down seedlings by mistake.

Whether you have several small beds or one large one, a fence defines a garden, protects it and ultimately makes it more productive. Solitude, as a spiritual discipline, is like the fence around the garden of your soul. It creates a space for other practices. Within the boundaries and protection of an island of solitude, you can pull out your other garden tools and begin to work the soil and sow the seeds that will result in spiritual fruit.

Without the boundaries of solitude our attempts at other disciplines like self-examination, silence, contemplative prayer, reflection and meditation are practically impossible. Without solitude, these other essential practices are likely to be crowded out, mowed down or just devoured by the needs of others. But how can we set those boundaries?

As my love for gardening has grown, so have the size of the beds in the back yard. Each year I keep turning under more of the lawn. My husband complains, as I said before, but I know if I'm going to have a productive garden, I've got to get rid of even good things, like lawn, to make space for vegetables or flowers.

The same is true of my spiritual life. I need to carve out some space in my busy, crowded days if I hope to harvest spiritual fruit. For me, staking out the garden of my soul begins with setting some boundaries around my time and devoting some of that time to solitude.

People often tell me they would love to tend to their spiritual life and plan to spend a lot of time in solitude and prayer. They hope they will be able to "get around to it" soon. I had a friend in high school who used to hand out wooden disks with the word "TUIT" printed on them. "You are always talking about all the things you'll do once you get 'a round TUIT,'" he'd say. "Here it is."

You may feel so stressed and busy that you only think of your spiritual life every once in a while, with a few pangs of guilt or even uncertainty. Whether we're busy with a demanding career, the never-ending needs of young children, the responsibilities of caring for an aging parent or just the daily grind of life, we say to ourselves, "Life is just crazy right now. But when I get around to it, I'll think more about spiritual things."

I know you do this, because I do it too. The truth is, life

rarely settles down on its own accord.

Why is it so hard to take action on our good intentions for cultivating the garden of our souls? It is, I think, because we have trouble staking out a garden. I have trouble with the fact that I will have to, at least temporarily, leave some other things undone or ask someone else to do them. I have trouble saying no, and I'm guessing, by looking at my friends' schedules, that they do too.

If I engage in cultivating the garden of my soul, I have to admit that I have needs (for rest, replenishment, growth) and that I want to have them met. My neediness makes me nervous. I'd rather focus on my capabilities and competencies. But admitting that I have needs motivates me to put up a fence, to set aside some space for myself.

I am convinced that many people, especially women, resign themselves to not having their needs met. They never even ask. I know I do this, especially when it comes to my need for solitude. Or I feel like solitude is something God wants me to do, so I'm meeting *his* need, not mine, by trying to find time for it.

But part of what keeps me from making time for solitude is that I really like having other people feel that I'm indispensable. I mean, I couldn't possibly leave my husband and children to their own devices, or put aside my work, even for a few hours. A lot of men I know (my husband included) feel great pressure to provide for their families (many women feel this, too), or that their job consumes who they are. They have trouble justifying time for themselves, trouble seeing themselves as anything beyond their job title.

In an effort to combat this tendency, as a spiritual discipline (and I recommend it to you), I take one long weekend off a year. The past two years I've gone to a writers' retreat in the mountains. As much as I love it, it is very hard to take the trip because I'm pretty sure things will totally fall apart at home and work without me there to hold them together. It's almost frustrating to see that my family and my clients do survive without me. And sinner that I am, I find it immensely gratifying to see the extra chaos that ensues in my absence.

But leaving my family and my work for a little while helps me gain perspective on my need to be needed.

You don't need to take a whole weekend off. Start with an hour or two. Put it on your calendar and say no to everyone and everything else for that time.

I have a friend who schedules solitude by drawing big green X's on her calendar. She stakes out time, and if someone asks her to get together or come to a meeting or do something on a green X day, she simply and graciously refuses.

Persist in staking out your garden. If your spouse won't or can't give you the time to be alone by taking over childcare and other household responsibilities for a few hours, pray for and seek out a solitude partner. A solitude partner is a spiritual friend who is also longing for time alone. One of my friends and I had watched each other's children for things such as work, doctor appointments or even just running errands. One day when we were talking about the desire both of us have to grow spiritually, I suggested we trade babysitting for times of solitude.

Set up one morning a week for each of you (or maybe, at first, it's one morning a month, or something a bit less structured). Drop off the kids after breakfast and pick them up again after lunch. If you don't have kids, or if they are older, take a day off from work or other obligations to just spend time with God. Make a date with him and let him set at least part of the agenda.

An Appointment with God

Say you have decided to make solitude a regular practice in your life. Or at least to give it a try. You've put it on your calendar, made an appointment with God. What do you do when you get to that appointment? How does this solitude thing work?

Solitude is time alone where you do very little. Get to a quiet place and just sit. You could read a bit of Scripture, journal or just sit. You don't really have to do anything, and in fact, I don't recommend trying to do an inductive Bible study or anything complicated. It may take all you've got to find a quiet place and to sit there. Solitude is mostly about being quiet and listening to what God might want to tell you. Maybe he'll tell you what he wants you to do, but he may just reassure you of his love.

My son is still young enough to enjoy just curling up in my lap. During a "cuddle time" we don't say much, but just sit on the couch or the La-Z-Boy, cuddling together. I kiss his hair and tell him I love him, rub his back. He tucks his head under my chin and rubs my arm. Sometimes we make little "uumm" noises to each other, like puppies. But mostly we are quiet. As he gets older, these times are becoming shorter and less frequent, but they are a treasure I hope I'm never too busy to engage in.

Sometimes Aaron will jump up and say, "Watch this, Mom!" and then he'll do some trick like stand on one foot, or try to skip, or proudly show me his latest Lego creation. "Great!" I'll say. But I don't love him more because he can do tricks or build a toy bulldozer. In fact, his tricks are not as important to me as his just being there is.

Likewise, sometimes time in solitude can be

time for you to spend on your Father's lap, just cuddling. God just wants to be with you, to hold you on his lap, so to speak. He will not love you more if you show him tricks or treasures. I know this, but I still find myself dragging out my accomplishments to try and impress him.

In other times of solitude God can tell you a story or teach you something in other ways. I happen to hear God best outside. Often God beckons me to the garden for times of solitude.

"The garden is a personal place of retreat and delight and labor for many people," writes Vigen Guroian. "Gardening helps them collect themselves, much like the activity of praying. For rich and poor—it does not make a difference—a garden is a place where body and soul are in harmony."

Sometimes, though, my garden is more labor than retreat, so I take to the woods for my appointments with God. I live in an area that has several public forest preserves nearby, with walking trails that wind through quiet fields and forests. I frequent them both alone and with my kids, in all seasons. Like Thoreau, I go there to discover what is truly important.

One snowy winter morning I left the kids with my friend and drove to a small nature preserve in the midst of a very busy, crowded suburb. It's an island of wilderness in a sea of strip malls. The weather was cold and cloudy. Snow had fallen overnight. I took the path through the meadow, walking slowly and stopping for a moment to admire puffs of snow caught in the skeletons of dried weeds, looking like cotton balls in rustic ring settings. But I didn't stop for long. The cold air kept me walking, moving.

The field was an old-fashioned photograph, pale snow and sepia prairie plants. Then a dab of color, looking like a bit of paint on the daguerreotype, caught my eye: a cluster of bright red berries clinging tenaciously to what appeared to be a dead vine. But it was not really dead. It looked to be dormant, yet it was bearing fruit: small but sturdy fruit that laughed at the cold and snow.

For me, being on a snowy prairie, seeing the fruit on a wizened vine in winter, was a way of hearing God. Lately my spiritual life had felt like that vine: dry and cold. Yet, God reminded me, I could still bear fruit. Not by my own power, or because of my circumstances; but by his power, in spite of my circumstances. He reminded me of this in the quiet.

You may shudder at the thought of a walk in a wintry woods. So don't go there. Sit by the fire with a blanket over your knees, go to a quiet chapel, sit on your patio and watch the birds, walk through a city park or go to the beach, but get alone. Don't do work, even gardening. Don't flip through a magazine. Just be. With God. That is how to do solitude.

A Quiet Place

Within the boundary of solitude we can cultivate our souls with the practice of silence. In silence, we garden with God. Sometimes we admire the flowers, thanking God for his goodness and creative abundance. Sometimes God shows us some weeds we hadn't seen before. Sometimes he will instruct us on what to plant. Sometimes it's just being: like walking with the Gardener through Eden in the cool of the evening.

Sometimes our longing for something profound in solitude and silence is not fully met. We have just an ordinary time, alone and quiet with God, dimly aware of his presence, but not much more than that. Such a time should not discourage us from gardening our soul. When the tomatoes are still green, it does not mean the plants are not productive.

If we are not quiet on a regular basis, we will not hear God's still, small voice. And listening for that voice is the heart of prayer, I am learning. When I engage in silence, I open up a space for conversation with God.

"People are meant to live in an on-going conversation with God, speaking and being spoken to," writes Dallas Willard in *Hearing God*. This conversation is the basis for our connection with God. "Our union with God—his presence with us, in which our aloneness is banished and the meaning and full purpose of human existence is realized—*consists chiefly in a conversational relationship with God while we are each consistently and deeply engaged as his friend and co-laborer in the affairs of the kingdom of the heavens.*"

A conversational relationship: what does that look like? In my life it means just shutting up for a while, to allow for quiet pauses throughout my day so that I can hear God speak. In the quiet conversation of prayer my "meaning and full purpose" is slowly, over time, revealed. So often I struggle because I don't know what to say to God. But if I only listen, I find he knows what to say to me.

When you practice silence, you need not say anything. But if you like, pray a simple prayer, like "Come, Lord Jesus," or "Speak, for your servant is listening." Then just sit and wait. And wait. And wait. When your mind wanders, relax and gently repeat your prayer. Or pray about what your mind wandered to, then gently return to quiet listening. If you like, picture Jesus seated next to you, sitting quietly. If you wait patiently, trusting him and not filling the silence with words, he will speak. Maybe not audibly or even in specific words. Ultimately silence is about trust. Do you trust God to reveal himself, to transform the silence from one that is uncomfortable to one that is peaceful?

It may be that what you need more than a word from God is a reassurance of his presence. Marjorie Thompson writes about contemplative prayer, a prayer that moves even deeper, beyond conversation to communion. Contemplative prayer is foundational to some denominations, while other groups have virtually ignored it, focusing on other (worthwhile) things. Even if this type of prayer is not familiar to you, it is worth learning about and experimenting with.

"In contemplation we move from communicating with God through speech to communing with God through the gaze of love," Thompson writes in *Soul Feast*. "Words fall away, and the most palpable reality is being present to the lover of our souls. . . . The sole purpose of contemplation is to adore and enjoy God, which glorifies divine love."

Do you believe it to be possible? Unless you venture away from the distractions of people and activity, beyond words and even beyond listening, into the quiet garden of solitude and silence, you will never know for certain.

The Results of Solitude and Silence

The fruit of love grows when I nurture it with both solitude and fellowship. When I have time apart from my kids, my husband, the people I lead in ministry, I am more ready to move toward them in love, to engage in fellowship with them. I need to balance these two things and feel comfortable and safe in each context. Each makes me appreciate the other. My experience of solitude is enriched by my experience of community, and vice versa.

"Only as we are within the fellowship can we be alone, and only he that is alone can live in the fellowship. Only in the fellowship do we learn to be rightly alone and only in aloneness do we learn to live rightly in the fellowship," writes Dietrich Bonhoeffer in *Life Together*. "Each by itself has profound pitfalls and perils. One who wants fellowship without solitude plunges into the void of words and feelings, and one who seeks solitude without fellowship perishes in the abyss of vanity, self-infatuation and despair. Let him who cannot be alone beware of community. Let him who is not in community beware of being alone."

His insights obviously apply to our life in the church, but also in our families: only he (or she) that is alone can live in the family. As a member of a family, as a parent, I need to be able to be alone, not just to regroup but as a discipline so that I don't become addicted to meeting the needs of others. When I make time to be alone, those who depend on me not only appreciate me in my absence, they stretch their capabilities because I am not there to take care of their every need. And I appreciate the community of my family much more when I have balanced my time with them with time alone.

Sometimes I can stake out longer times of solitude, but sometimes I have to creatively weave it into the fabric of my day. I'll spend a few moments in quiet reflection before I get out of bed. After making a sack lunch for Melanie and quizzing her on her

math, I'll go up to my office and have a few moments to just sit and jot a sentence or two in my journal. Then, Aaron will awaken and come and climb on my lap. We'll cuddle, then I'll get him breakfast and throw in a load of laundry, then return to my office for a few more minutes of alone time. While sometimes I need to get away from my kids for more than a few minutes,

sometimes I have to just take what I can get. I'd like to pray, uninterrupted, but I wouldn't trade Aaron on my lap, fresh from sleep, for anything.

Silence and solitude make the garden of my soul a more peaceful place. Think about it: we all long for peace and quiet. Do we ever stop to think that if we got quiet, we might find some peace? When I visit my in-laws' lake home in the country, away from the noise of the city, I am always struck by the quiet. It's so peaceful up there. Silence and solitude cultivate peace.

In Jill Murphy's whimsical children's picture book, *Five Minutes Peace*, she describes the quandary Mrs. Large (a mommy elephant with three boisterous elephant children) finds herself in. Most mommies, large and small, can relate to her frustration as she goes through her house, from the kitchen and even to the bathtub to try and stay a few steps ahead of her demanding children for "just five minutes peace." Mrs. Large is searching for peace and eventually (but only after all three kids end up in the tub with her) finds a few minutes to sneak away.

It's a funny book for kids, but I know I've felt a lot like Mrs. Large. I just want a little peace. But peace is more than just the absence of noise or interruption. It's more than hiding in the bathtub and muttering, "Take me away . . ."

When the Bible talks about peace, it's more than just the absence of conflict. Often it has to do with community: not just getting along with others but connecting with them, and connecting with God.

Jesus, just before his death, told his disciples what to expect: a helper who would walk alongside them, a constant divine presence. "But the Counselor, the Holy Spirit, whom the Father will send in my name, will teach you all things and will remind you of everything I have said to you. Peace I leave with you; my peace I give you. I do not give to you as the world gives. Do not let your hearts be troubled and do not be afraid" (John 14:26-27).

What is this peace that is unique to Jesus, unlike what the world calls peace? It is his Spirit, his ongoing and very real presence in our day-to-day lives. We do not need to be afraid, for his presence makes wherever we are a safe place.

Is the fruit of peace growing in the garden of your soul? The peace "that passes understanding," that comes not because of, but in spite of, our circumstances?

When we engage in the practice of solitude and silence, we come into the presence of God, and there we find peace, because he *is* peace.

Digging deeper

1. What boundaries do you need to establish in order to practice the discipline of solitude? What keeps you from setting those boundaries?

2. Being alone is frightening for many people. If solitude frightens you, spend some time journaling about what specifically you are afraid of. For example, you might be afraid that you'll be bored, or that God might not show up. Or you might be afraid that he will.

3. Would you describe your life as peaceful? If not full of peace, is there just a little peace somewhere? What steps could you take to help peace flourish?

4

Mess

Connecting with God
Through Other People

Gardens are not made by singing,
"Oh, how beautiful," and sitting in the shade.

<small>RUDYARD KIPLING</small>

One of the best things I can do for a garden, even before I plant anything in it, is not only to work the soil, but to add fertilizer or compost to it. Compost is yard clippings, vegetable peelings, coffee grounds and other organic garbage, allowed (with the help of earthworms) to decompose into soil-like matter that is rich in nutrients. Technically it's called "humus." Gardeners call it "black gold."

The narrow border along my front walk was crowded with irises, which had not been divided for many years. Doses of fertilizer had been few and far between. As a result, the soil was depleted, and the irises had few blooms and were mostly just spiky green leaves, some of them even turning brown.

"The first thing you need to do is to clear out half of these plants, then add lots of poop," declared my friend Cathi, another gardening guru, as she stood looking at the bed. We spent an afternoon dividing the irises and moving some to the other side of the yard. Much of the soil was rock hard clay, so we dug some of it out. Then we dumped several bags of composted cow manure into the small bed. Once we had removed some of the irises and amended the soil, we added a few new plants. That fall I put in some tulip bulbs.

The next spring, when I would drive up to our house and

look at the profusion of blooms that lined the sidewalk, it made me catch my breath. I experienced an unusual amount of joy for such a small garden.

Gardening, for all the beauty it produces, requires us to get rather messy. We cannot just sit in the shade and admire it, as Kipling notes. It requires getting down on your hands and knees and working with the soil, manure and compost. In a given afternoon in the garden I will encounter (and often have to pick up) earthworms, slugs and other bugs. I'll most likely get dirt under my fingernails, get my garden gloves dirty and soaked by the leaky hose, stain the knees of my jeans, and probably accidentally track mud into the kitchen when I go in for a glass of ice water. By definition, gardening is a dirty job. But I enjoy it, and not just the results: while flowers and vegetables are a satisfying reward, there is a joy that comes just from interacting with the planet so intimately. Even getting dirty makes me feel joyful. I read recently that the average American spends 93 percent of her time inside. My goal in life is to single-handedly lower that average.

What will enrich the soil of your soul?

Asking for Help

When I page through old personal journals, considering seasons past, the most fruitful were those marked by authentic (but often complicated) interaction with other people. God's most effective agents of grace, and of growth, are his people.

Sometimes the growth comes when other people wound us, or when we realize that we have wounded them. Conflict is inevitable. But wrestling with and resolving the conflict helps my soul's garden to flourish.

Part of resolving conflict involves admitting our mistakes

and forgiving others for theirs. James 5:16 says to "confess your faults to one another." We need others to help us see the weeds we can't see and to help us pull them from the garden of our souls. Just talking to God about it is not enough. God speaks to us through others, and if we are alone in our spiritual journey, we are more likely to get lost along the way.

Sadly many people feel they can grow spiritually all by themselves, or perhaps by reading self-help books, or books like the one you are reading right now. Certainly reading is helpful, just as reading gardening books helps me in my efforts to grow tomatoes or flowers. But no book can walk through my garden and tell me where to move the yarrow, or share with me cuttings or divisions from their own garden and offer advice on where to plant each one. To really grow, we need the help of others, either in a group or one-on-one.

The discipline of confession is the most effective means of growth when it happens within the context of an established, trusting friendship, with the purpose of healing. A small group or spiritual mentoring relationship is ideal for this type of thing. But sometimes it's just someone you can be real with.

The sins I struggle with, the insecurities I battle, I can't battle alone. So I call my best friend. She doesn't condemn me; she simply listens and shares her struggles as well. We end up feeling glad that both of us are far from perfect, because we'd both be really boring and annoying people if we were.

Sometimes the discipline of confession means we must tell someone, a trusted fellow traveler, what sin we see in our own life. Sometimes, though, we cannot see our sins, and we need to invite our trusted friend into the garden of our souls and allow them to point out the thistles that we have convinced ourselves are just a spiny strain of lavender.

A trusted confessor can also help us to put things in better order. Stopping by my house one spring day, Gina studied my backyard perennial bed with her practiced eye. "You have a lot of good stuff here," she says, indicating the peonies that were nearly done blooming and the Shasta daisies that were in bud. "You just need to move things around. After the peonies are done, divide them and put half over here. Divide the daisies now and put some here. Move the yarrow completely to the back; it's too tall to be in front."

Move plants? What a concept! I'd thought once they had roots they couldn't be disturbed. But move them I did, early in the spring, and they even bloomed that summer.

Gina's objective view of my haphazard garden helped me to see it in a new way. Her experience helped my hodgepodge efforts to move steadily in the direction of balance and beauty. With her help I realized I didn't need more plants; I only needed to rearrange the plants I had.

In our spiritual lives we sometimes need the help of a more experienced person. To learn what needs to be pulled, divided or moved around in our lives so that we can thrive. Sometimes simplifying or just rearranging my life, rather than adding more activities or possessions or accomplishments to it, can make it more productive and more beautiful. But we often need an objective opinion to help us figure out what needs to be done.

Inviting experts like Cathi or Gina into my garden improved it because they were willing to tell me about what kind of changes would make the garden more beautiful and productive. They were even willing to work beside me to help things grow. Because I trusted their gardening wisdom, I was willing to listen.

Likewise, inviting other people into the garden of my soul has made my life richer and more fruitful. Whether it's being discipled by a more experienced Christian or spending some time in a counselor's office, asking for help is essential.

Relationships, especially long-term ones, add texture and meaning and significance to our lives. The people who strengthen and build you up and fill you with joy, the difficult people who test your patience and drain you, and everyone who defies such simple categories: they all provide essential nutrients for the garden of your soul.

And yet, if I put fertilizer on my flowers every day, I'd do more harm than good. Too much can be harmful. For example, last summer my husband decided to put a combination of weed killer and fertilizer on our lawn. He filled the spreader and went back and forth across the front yard. A few days later, the clover and dandelions were gone, and some grass was thriving, but some spots (where he had turned the corner with the spreader and given the grass a double dose of Weed-'n-Feed) were burned yellow. He realized that too much of a good thing is not a good thing.

Likewise, the garden of my soul needs both the fertilizer of community and the rest of solitude to thrive. Jesus, during his ministry on earth, certainly engaged in deep community with his followers, but he also practiced solitude on a regular basis. The pattern of his life, and one I want to emulate as his follower, was to engage deeply both in community and in solitude.

True community respects each person's need for solitude and is nourished corporately by each individual's private experience of God. My strongest, most loving friendships have been ones where I have felt respect and a balance between closeness and space, where I have acknowledged that I am alone and yet connected.

In solitude, we set up a fence around the garden of our souls. We create an island. There we invite God to work the soil, to plant and water. When we ask others for help, when we enter into community, we can really begin to grow. Community ushers others into the garden, and like fertilizer, they bring a richness to the soil of our soul that mere plowing cannot. With that richness, however, comes an inevitable mess. Connecting with others is a gift, but you have to get your hands dirty to receive it.

Made for Community

God has always existed in triune community—Father, Son and Holy Spirit—mutually submitting and serving and loving each other. We were created to do the same. Genesis 1:26 says, "Then God said, 'Let us make man in *our* image, in *our* likeness'" (italics mine).

"According to Scripture, community is not a human invention or a mere social convention, or even less a solution of desperation for group survival," writes Gilbert Bilezikian. "Community is God's dearest creation because it is grounded in his nature and reflects his true identity as a plurality of persons in oneness of being. Moreover, the establishment of community was God's dream for his creation from the very beginning, and he has pursued it all along history and will continue to do so to the very end of time."

We were created to reflect the image of the community that is God's nature, and a defining characteristic of true Christian community is service. Jesus told us to humble ourselves and serve others, so that we would grow in his kingdom. And when we are served by others, it is also humbling, because we must face squarely the fact that we are not entirely self-sufficient.

"I love the fact that the word *humus* — the decayed vegetable matter that feeds the roots of plants — comes from the same root that gives rise to the word *humility*. It is a blessed etymology," writes Parker Palmer. To humble myself, without it turning into prideful false humility, I find it best to concentrate not on my own humility, but on the other person's needs: What will feed the soil of their soul?

"The physical presence of other Christians is a source of incomparable joy and strength to the believer," writes Dietrich Bonhoeffer. And this is mostly true. It would be hard to live a fruitful spiritual life in isolation. If you look at Paul's description of a Spirit-filled person in Galatians, you notice all of the characteristics of the fruit of the Spirit are best expressed in community. Kindness and gentleness are not virtues if you never interact with another person. Patience blooms when you have to live shoulder to shoulder with people who annoy you. And although we often hear self-help gurus say, "Be gentle to yourself," gentleness is best demonstrated through the way I respond to someone else, especially if that person is being less than gentle with me.

So many of the Bible's exhortations are about what we should say or do to "one another," not simply to ourselves. "Be tenderhearted, forgiving one another," writes Paul in Ephesians 4:32, and in Colossians 3:16 he adds: "Let the word of Christ dwell in you richly as you teach and admonish one another with all wisdom." We learn what Jesus is like by being loved in his name by others.

Investing in the Soil

This fall the local garden center ran out of bagged manure, so I went to a local riding stable where a big "Free Fertilizer" sign hangs on the side of the barn. I took my shovel and several plastic bags and helped myself from the manure pile. (The experience brought back memories of working at a stable when I was eleven years old, where I traded my "expertise" with a pitchfork for riding lessons.)

I loaded three heavy-duty garbage bags of well-rotted (meaning old, not fresh, and hence, not as smelly) manure into the back of the mini-van, drove home with the windows open, then emptied the bags into a new garden bed where I hope to plant vegetables in the spring. While it was not a fun chore, I know that the fertilizer I work into the soil this fall will reap great benefits to the garden next spring.

You may be in a spiritual season of life where you feel like all you're doing is shoveling manure, be it in your church or your family or your job. Every part of your spiritual life feels like dirty work. You may feel that nothing is blooming in the garden of your soul. But no garden blooms in every season. Even spring, with all its promise of new life and growth, is muddy and messy. So if you find yourself in a humble season, take heart—God is going to grow great things in the soil of your soul.

Community is often untidy and humbling. Sometimes people disappoint us. Their actions do not show us anything about Jesus; in fact, they may seem to show us anything *but* that. It is not always easy to live in community. People are messy. They and their issues, problems and habits are complicated, an annoying mixture of good and bad motives and actions. They seem to mess up our lives, bringing chaos rather than order.

When I am doing life with other people, I become aware not only of their weaknesses, but also of my own. My mother and I, for example, are close friends, although we live two thousand miles apart. But sometimes our insecurities overlap and we wound each other. It happened this morning, in a phone conversation fraught with misunderstanding, and I was sad and headachy and resentful for most of the day.

But this evening she e-mailed an epistle of love and wisdom and confession and forgiveness. I cried, suddenly aware of my own stubbornness and insecurity, but also thankful for my mom's willingness to pursue community, to not give up on our relationship, to strengthen our connection. Our conflict, and the subsequent resolution of that conflict, enriched the soil of my soul. Accepting the fact of our own and others' imperfection is a part of growth.

"To forgive other people for being able to give you only a little love—that's a hard discipline," Henri Nouwen writes. "To keep asking others for forgiveness because you can give only a little love—that's a hard discipline, too."

While God wants us to dwell in community, he knows that human beings will never completely fulfill all the longings of our heart. We are full of a longing that only God can meet, and that he wants to meet. The best type of community is one where I receive love (even imperfect human love), but don't necessarily get all my needs met. The richest community points us toward the healing love of God, reminds me that I am still broken and needy and hungry for God. The best community realizes its own limitations and respects the fact that each of us needs both to be alone with God and together with others.

"The key to this form of community involves holding a paradox—the paradox of having relationships in which we protect each other's aloneness," writes Parker Palmer. "We must come together in ways that respect the solitude of the soul."

After ten years as a small group leader, I have seen what happens when we do not protect each other's aloneness. Often it results in awkward attempts to change the little things that annoy us about one other. The motive, in most groups, for "fixing" is to prevent conflict. This does not always work, of course. But sometimes it appears to, and the conflict goes underground and seems not to be there. But then it reemerges as a sort of inertia where we become bored or resentful that God has put us here with these difficult, shallow people. If we want to see the garden of our souls flourish, we need to be thankful for the messiness of community, the sometimes difficult or just grindingly ordinary daily interactions that, over time, will enrich the soil of our soul.

People are a source of both joy and pain. Connecting with others, through your family, your church, your prayer group, your twelve-step group, your neighborhood, wherever, brings you into the community you were made for. In that place God uses those messy, imperfect people to fertilize your soul. They minister to you, you minister to them, and both the joy and the pain act as fertilizer to help us grow.

Using Your Gifts

What exactly do we *do* in community that enriches the soil of our souls? How can we find that meaningful connection? By focusing on what we can give to others, because of what God has given to us.

Within the context of community, I can gain much by giving much. When I engage in serving others, in putting others first, be it in my neighborhood, at church or at home, I work fertilizer into the soil of my soul. Serving others is not glamorous, but it adds a richness and fruitfulness to my soul's garden that few other things can.

When I serve others, fruit begins to develop. By acting in a loving way, I become more loving. By showing them kindness, I become more kind.

If we serve in a way that reflects how God made us, we are more likely to grow. There are many ways to serve, and I find that the service that makes me feel closest to God, that enhances my relationship with him, is service that reflects my spiritual gifts. Romans 12:6 says, "We have different gifts, according to the grace given us." You have a gift and you should use it. If you have the gift of encouragement, take some time each week to jot a note to someone. It may not even feel like "serving," but it is a way to engage in community that will nourish the garden of your soul.

I know that I am more likely to grow if I'm taking care of, even in a small way, someone besides myself. Not that I should ignore my own needs, but to balance meeting them with helping others.

The Bible also says we should not try to be something we are not. We should not serve in a way that does not fit who God made us to be. For example, our church has a decorating team that gets together to create wonderful projects like centerpieces, Christmas decorations, all kinds of crafty things that are used around the church throughout the year. I have several friends who are a part of this team. They serve the whole body by making our church a more beautiful place.

I am not on this team.

I have no desire to be on this team.

No one has ever invited me to be on it.

That's because they don't want me to be on it. It's nothing personal. It's just that I am craft-impaired. I know this about myself. It's fairly obvious to other people. If I tried to join this team and serve God there, thinking I'd get extra points with him because it was so difficult for me, I'd be dead wrong. Also, I wouldn't be helping the church. I'd be making a mess, getting in the way and feeling frustrated.

As far as I can tell thus far, God wants me shepherding people toward fuller devotion to him, through writing, through teaching, through leading groups. That's what will not only help others but will bring me both growth and joy. So that's what I try my best to do. I do it at my church, I do it at home with my children, I do it as I sit and write and rewrite the paragraphs you are reading. I don't always get it exactly right; in fact, sometimes I make a mess. But that's okay.

Do you know what your purpose is? Do you know how your gifts play into that? How much time have you invested in finding the answers to those questions? "When we set out to discover a life purpose, we embark on a journey within, for to understand our reason for being is to recognize the shape of our souls," writes Judith Couchman.

Read, study, spend time alone with God, so that you can eventually "recognize the shape of your soul." Do whatever you can to figure out what your purpose, your calling, your spiritual gifts. Then arrange your life so that you can fulfill your purpose, follow your calling, use your spiritual gifts. (If you have young children, your purpose and calling are at least in part related to their discipleship and care.) But no matter where you use your gifts, employing them will help you to grow. The soil of your soul will be rich.

Bringing It Home

Each morning I get up with my kids, make them breakfast, get them juice, put a video on for them, help them get dressed . . . There are times I wish I could just sit, read the paper and drink my coffee. Or maybe read my Bible and pray. There are times I don't even get as far as wishing. I'm just on auto-pilot. Flip on the coffee maker, drop the frozen waffles in the toaster, fill the sippy cups. I could do it in my sleep. Sometimes it's so early I feel like I am, for all practical purposes, still asleep.

But if I view my morning routine as an act of worship, it can be transformed into an expression of love: to God, to my kids, to my husband. It can be as "spiritual" as a Bible study. It's easy to forget, but getting the kids breakfast is an opportunity to express love, and therefore, help the fruit of love to grow in my life. Through humble service, through being fully present as I pour the cereal and listen to early morning chatter of my kids, I can grow spiritually before I even open my Bible.

As my pastor John Ortberg says, "God is not just interested in your 'spiritual' life. He's just interested in your *life*."

It's easy to think of the discipline of service as something we do outside the home, with the label "volunteer work," or in some cases "job." We don't think of our work at home as service, but that's what it is.

Shortly after my son was born, I had two children in diapers and the workload felt overwhelming. I remember writing a letter of complaint to God in my journal. "What am I supposed to be, some kind of slave?"

When I got quiet for a moment, I realized the answer was yes. Because that's what Jesus came to do, "not to be served, but to serve." The apostle Paul even described himself as a "bondservant of Jesus Christ." If we think of ourselves as serving only people, and not serving Christ through them, I think it's easier to complain and harder to stay motivated. But when I read Christ's words about "whoever wants to be first must be the servant of all," I need to remember that they apply not only to volunteer work at church but also to my family.

The Hidden Benefits of Quiet Service

Our connection in community is transformed by service. Likewise, our service in community is transformed by secrecy. But in a self-promotional culture, to do good and simply refrain from mentioning it is one of the hardest disciplines. As a mom whose resume has a few gaps in it, I often feel the need to bolster my self-image with a list of my accomplishments. Sometimes when I have done some small act of service, I find a way to casually mention it to other people. And often when I feel led to pray for someone, I make sure I remember to tell them about it.

While prayer and service are disciplines that will undoubtedly produce fruit in the garden of my life, the Bible warns against pride that comes from doing our good works "before men." When what others think of me becomes more important to me than who I am in God's eyes, it is time to engage for a while in the discipline of secrecy. Secrecy is the cure for pride. Secrecy, applied to prayer, service and other practices, is like a fertilizer that multiplies the spiritual blessings and enriches the soil of our souls.

Secrecy is especially hard for me to practice in my marriage. Scot and I have a favorite fight, with many variations. I call it, "Who works harder?" Because I work from home and spend most of my time looking after the kids and the house, he thinks I have it easier. For the very same reason, I think I have the tougher assignment. We compare to-do lists and who did what, when. If I were to do something for him and not point it out to him, I wonder what would happen?

John Ortberg writes that most of us are addicted to the approval of others. We want to be noticed, which is not necessarily bad, but we want it so much that we spend an inordinate amount of time on image management. Ortberg writes that the discipline of secrecy is "an enormously helpful practice for gaining freedom from this addiction."

Jesus recommended that when we give money, fast or pray, we don't need to let anyone else know about it. Jesus said of the Pharisees, who boasted of their good works, that men's attention was all the reward they would get. But for those who do good works in secret, who pray in a closet and don't reveal what goes on there, he promises God's favor and reward.

There have been a few times I've given small financial gifts anonymously. This gave me great joy. But for some reason it's easier for me to give anonymously than to pray anonymously.

Often when I sit down to pray, I feel intense concern for certain people. I sometimes ask God who to pray for and then pray for whomever he brings to mind. Other times I just know that a specific friend or even acquaintance needs my intercession. I'm energized and excited by the opportunity to pray for people.

But recently I noticed that telling people about my prayers for them began, very subtly, to become almost as important as the praying itself. Now, it is not wrong to encourage someone by letting them know about your intercessions on their behalf. As I have the spiritual gift of encouragement, my natural inclination is to encourage people by letting them know of my prayers. But not long after I began telling everyone how jazzed I was to intercede for them, I stumbled across this quote: "Intercession is the most intensely social act that the human being is capable of," writes Douglas V. Steere in *Dimensions of Prayer.* "When it is carried on secretly, it is mercifully preserved from, in fact, almost immunized against, the possible corruptions to which all outer deeds of service for others are subject."

Corruptions? Who, me? I realized that some weeds of pride were cropping up in my prayer life, that I needed a little fertilizer, a little dose of secrecy. I was reminded that serving others, whether in your family, your neighborhood or your church, doesn't just help other people, it fertilizes the garden of your soul, making it flourish—especially if you don't draw attention to it.

Multiplying by Dividing

One of the most wonderful things about gardening, especially if you have perennials, is that your garden does better if you share.

Perennials don't die but go dormant in winter, then reemerge, bigger and better, each growing season. A single plant, over time, will become a large clump of many stems with a mass of roots. The best course of action to keep the plant healthy and fill in your flower bed is to divide the plant.

Most perennials thrive on division, a necessary chore that often intimidates amateur gardeners. They don't want to dig up a healthy plant and chop it in half. Some plants with fibrous roots require a strong chop with an axe to come apart.

Here is the lovely paradox: when you divide your plants, they multiply. When you split a plant in half or quarters, you can replant one part in the same spot, and another part can be replanted elsewhere in your garden, another given to a friend. Likewise, when we give of ourselves, we create room for our hearts to grow. When we love others, love blooms more vigorously in us.

My gardens over the years have been enhanced by divisions given me by friends and strangers. Cathi brought a seemingly innocuous pot of yarrow, which literally took over the perennial bed. I kept dividing it and giving it away, only to have it grow back even more abundantly. Gina gave me columbine; my neighbor across the street gave me dalia bulbs. My garden has become more beautiful and also more meaningful: each plant is a reminder of the person who shared it with me. When I see the columbine blooming, I feel gratitude, not just for the flowers, but for my long-time friendship with Gina.

Once I was driving through my neighborhood when I saw a hand-lettered sign on a mailbox: "Free flowers." I looked into the yard and saw that the owner had a huge border of pale purple irises and had been busy dividing the plants. A pile nearly five foot wide of unwanted irises sat in the middle of her lawn.

I pulled into the driveway, and she loaded me up with not only irises but some lily of the valley as well. I took them home and planted them in various spots around my own yard.

The garden of your soul will flourish if you embrace this paradox of multiplying by dividing. When you give to others in community, you receive.

The Soil's Purpose
As I write this, it is April outside, cool and misty one minute,

warm and damp the next, but almost always some kind of wet.

As I walked to the bus stop with my daughter this morning, I was struck by the scent of the air. It smelled like dirt and earthworms and grass waking up. It smelled of spring. I kept inhaling through my nose, snuffling it up. It was almost intoxicating. Around here winters are so cold that scents seem to be suspended, frozen. So we don't just notice spring by the weather or the greening of the grass but with our noses.

The smell of it creates in me an urge to garden. I have a strong desire to put on my old ripped gardening jeans (for gardening, as we've said, is messy) and get out and plant something in the good soil I have worked hard to create. In fall I add manure to the soil. In spring I start turning over the soil in the beds, working and loosening it, adding compost or fertilizer wherever it's needed. God works with me outdoors as well, sending spring rains to soften and nourish the earth.

But healthy soil is the means, not the end, for a gardener. I need to put something in it: A companion or two for the crocuses, which are blooming, brave and lonely, in the front yard. Herbs and vegetables in the back yard. Some pansies in the pots on the porch.

I have worked and fertilized the soil for a reason: so that I can sow seeds and they will thrive. That's the whole point of a garden. If we stop before we plant, we don't have a garden. We just have really good dirt.

As I work the soil of my soul, fertilizing and strengthening it, I realize that I have made it ready for seeds, which will become plants, which will flower and bear fruit. To stop now would defeat my purpose.

It is time for planting.

Digging deeper

1. How often do you ask for help with your spiritual life? Do you have anyone in your life who can mentor or encourage you spiritually? If not, what steps could you take to find someone? Also, what steps could you take to initiate a relationship where you can help someone else?

2. "To forgive other people for being able to give you only a little love—that's a hard discipline," Henri Nouwen writes. What gets in the way of being able to forgive others for their inadequacies? Can you think of a time when you were able to give only a little love? How did that affect your experience of community?

3. Have you ever served someone and not told them? How would engaging in the discipline of secrecy affect the garden of your soul? What are some ways you could secretly serve your closest friends or family members?

5

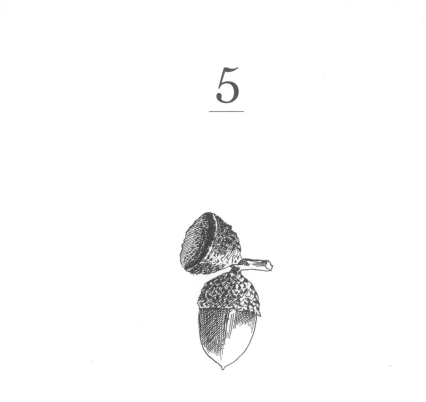

Seed

Hearing and Obeying
God's Word

The very act of planting a seed in the earth
has in it to me something beautiful.
I always do it with a joy that is largely mixed with awe.
I watch my garden beds after they are sown,
and think how one of God's exquisite miracles is going on
beneath the dark earth out of sight.

CELIA THAXTER

April really is, as T. S. Eliot observed, the cruelest month, especially for a gardener in the Midwest. Two weeks ago it was nearly eighty degrees for several days. Last night we had frost and temperatures in the twenties. Today we had snow. This weekend it's supposed to be seventy-five again.

While crocuses and even the daffodils can handle these wild weather swings, more delicate specimens cannot. I cannot yet plant impatiens or other "tender annuals," tempted as I might be on warm days. But about a month from now, it will be the proper time to plant them.

Everything needs to be planted in season. The bulbs I planted last fall are blooming now. I can plant gladiolus bulbs in the spring, and they'll be blooming by summer. Why is it that tulip bulbs need five months in the cold ground and glads or other summer bulbs need only three in the gradually warming soil? Because God made each of them unique.

Some seeds need a blast of cold to germinate. In February, when my garden is a jumble of dead stalks and icy mud, it's ideal planting weather—for poppies. I scatter them on the snow, or just scratch the top layer of frozen earth and drop them. Planting in February? Wouldn't it be better to wait until it's warmer?

Well, it would be if I were planting tomatoes. But poppy seeds need cold. So it's not just that it's *okay* to plant them in winter—it is the optimum time to plant them. If I wait until it's warmer, the poppies may not bloom at all.

In a garden you have to know when to plant what. In various seasons I plant different things. In February, poppies. In October, tulip bulbs.

In the garden of your soul God will plant the right thing in the right season. When we try to rush things, we wind up getting hurt. Some seeds need to stay in the ground longer. Often before a seed becomes a seedling, it begins sending roots down deep into the soil. Likewise, the most important growth in the garden of your soul may occur underground, unseen.

The Bible often refers to God's Word as a seed, and just as I know the best time to plant my seeds, God knows the correct season for different words that he plants: a word of correction in a season of rebellion, a word of comfort in a season of pain, a "well done" when we have pleased him.

God knows what needs to be planted at what time, and it's very freeing for me to realize that the impulse that draws me to a certain passage of Scripture, or brings a verse to mind at a certain time is often a divine one. But I must go to God's Word if I want fruit to grow in my garden. I must seek truth and allow God to plant it: through reading the Bible, through listening and learning from teachers at church, on the radio, through reading books that help me to grow spiritually.

We've seen that much of the success of a garden depends on the soil and whether it has been worked and fertilized and prepared. In Luke 8 Jesus tells a parable about a farmer who encounters a variety of soil conditions. Some seeds land on the path where he walks, but they are quickly stepped on and eaten by birds before they can sprout. Some seed falls on rocky soil and sprouts, but then quickly dies for lack of moisture that good soil provides. Some of the seed falls into a patch of thorny weeds, and although the seed sprouts, the seedlings are quickly choked out.

"Still other seed fell on good soil. It came up and yielded a crop, a hundred times more than was sown" (v. 8).

When his disciples asked him to explain the parable, Jesus replied, "This is the meaning of the parable: The seed is the word of God" (v. 11). Jesus explains the analogies he's making with the path, the rocky soil, the thorny soil. There are many things that can keep God's word from taking root in the garden of our souls.

So what happens when the soil of our heart is plowed, fertilized and ready for planting? Then our lives can be fruitful. Jesus tells his disciples, "But the seed on good soil stands for those with a noble and good heart, who hear the word, retain it, and by persevering produce a crop" (v. 15).

How do we produce a crop? Not by trying really hard to be fruitful. Instead, it's about focusing on preparing the soil. Jesus says that a spiritually fruitful life begins with cultivating a heart that is noble and good, by hearing God's Word, by retaining it and by persevering.

Goodness Begins with Abiding

How do we cultivate "a noble and good heart"? If you've tried to be good and noble through your own efforts, you know that it's pretty close to impossible. We've learned that a tree can't bear fruit on its own.

However, if you allow the Master Gardener to work the soil of your heart, if you stake out the garden boundaries with the discipline of solitude and enrich the soil with true community, you will have soil that is ready to receive the seed of God's Word.

Jesus was the ultimate model of a "noble and good heart." He calls us to live as he did, to abide in him. And that is where spiritual fruitfulness begins: in staying connected with God. When Jesus was here on earth, he practiced solitude and service. He ordered his life in a way that would strengthen his connection with his Father: time alone in prayer, time with people he loved, time serving others and healing and helping.

He lived this way for two reasons. First, he wanted to give us a living example, a demonstration of how to follow his command to abide. He used parables that cut to the heart of the issues, that made truth clear to both the simple and the wise. But the best illustration he ever gave was his own life, because the way he lived showed us what deep connection with God looks like: "If you obey my commands, you will remain in my love, just as I have obeyed my Father's commands and remain in his love" (John 15:10).

Beyond being an example, Jesus cultivated his soul's garden with spiritual practices like solitude and service. Why? Because Jesus was and is an eternal being. Before his earthly existence he had always lived in deep communion with his Father. He simply desired to continue to live in that strong connection.

Following his example, living every part of our lives the way he did (not just the more public parts) makes abiding in him seem like the only logical thing to do. Engaging in spiritual practices that Jesus did will strengthen our connection to the vine.

"Asking ourselves 'What would Jesus do?' when suddenly in the face of an important situation simply is not an adequate discipline or preparation to enable one to live as he lived," writes

Dallas Willard. "The secret of the easy yoke, then, is to learn from Christ how to live our total lives, how to invest all our time and our energies of mind and body as he did."

In other words, if I want to be patient with my kids or with an annoying coworker, I can't wait until they're driving me crazy to decide to start acting like Jesus. I have to get alone and get quiet long before I encounter difficult situations, just as Jesus did, if I want to have the strength to act like him in those trying times. In times of intense ministry, the Bible often notes, Jesus went away to quiet places and prayed.

When we live our lives following Jesus' example, we are likely to cultivate a noble and good heart, one which will be open to hearing God's Word.

Hearing the Word

Reading and studying the Bible is a core spiritual practice that will strengthen our spiritual roots. I have a friend who is going through a very tough time, and she feels like God is very far away from her and her troubles. "I wish he would just speak to me," she declares.

How often when we are at this point (and we've all been there—or will be someday) do we pick up God's Word to us, the Bible, and just read it? Why, when I'm struggling and wanting a word from God, do I forget
to read the Word? I call the Bible "God's
Word," but when I am despairing, I often
think of it as something remote, distant or
irrelevant.

But really, his Word, the Bible, is a love letter,
a personal epistle with truth and comfort and
correction that can speak directly to my life and

my situation. God knows and understands what the garden of my soul needs, and if I let him, he will plant what is needed to make it a place of beauty and fruitfulness.

Another friend of mine used to work at a Christian bookstore. Often customers would come in and announce that they had just become a Christian. "I'm looking for a book that will kind of sum up the essentials of the faith," they'd say.

"Well, we recommend the Bible," my friend would reply.

"No, no, I just want a book that kind of explains the basics," the new Christian would reply.

"Well, let me show you our Bibles," my friend would say patiently.

"No, no, that's not what I'm looking for!" they would respond.

What were they expecting? Maybe Cliffs Notes?

Even if we have been a part of God's family for a while, we sometimes look for information or answers everywhere except the place that they are—in God's Word: "All of Scripture is God-breathed and is useful for teaching, rebuking, correcting and training in righteousness," Paul wrote to his protégé Timothy (2 Timothy 3:16).

Often I'm more interested in the comfort of the Psalms than in the rebuking or correcting parts. But sometimes God needs to plant a seed of correction. If I want the garden of my soul to flourish, I've got to allow the Master Gardener to plant his Word there. I've got to read and study the Bible, listen to teaching or read books that will help it germinate.

Digging Deep

"I really want to read the whole Bible, and I'm getting there, but Chronicles is so boring," confided a woman in the class I teach at church. "But I'm going to get through it!"

"Why?" I asked.

"That's what Christians should do, read the whole Bible, so I'm working on it really hard."

Her comments depressed me, as I had just taught a lesson on reflective reading. I had challenged my students to focus on a few verses and meditate on them, rather than skimming quickly through a whole chapter. It appeared I hadn't quite gotten through to her. I had told my class to focus on quality, and she seemed to be focusing on quantity.

Chronicles, or any other book in the Old or New Testament, can and does speak into our lives. Just look at Bruce Wilkinson's popular book *The Prayer of Jabez*, which is based on just two verses in Chronicles, 1 Chronicles 4:9-10.

Wilkinson knew the importance of reading and letting God's Word speak into his life. His book is about how those two verses instructed him to pray and the impact it had on his life and his ministry. But often we don't read the Bible in that way. We want simply to be done reading, rather than to be transformed. When we read in this way, we often miss the message, and our garden soil gets hard packed, like the path in Jesus' parable, so that truth does not sink in and take root.

My student, although she was eager to learn, probably couldn't begin to tell you what Chronicles was even about, let alone how it related to her life. Nevertheless, she was bound and determined to finish reading it.

As we spoke further, I realized that part of why this new Christian wanted to read the whole Bible was because her daughter, who was not a believer, had a lot of questions that my friend did not know how to answer. She hoped that reading through the Bible would enable her to not only answer her daughter's questions but ultimately would allow her to lead her daughter to faith. While her goal was admirable and understandable, her method of achieving it was likely to fail.

But I fall into the same trap. I think, *If I just read this book, or study this chapter, I'll be able to live a fruitful life. My soul's garden will flower in just the way I plan.* But like any garden, my soul's garden will often benefit from my letting go of my obsessive attempts to control the results of cultivation.

Good gardeners know this, and I can learn something from a physical garden that will help my soul's garden flourish. Gardener Mirabel Osler writes:

> The very soul of a garden is shriveled by zealous regimentation. . . . Control is vital for the original design and form; and a ruthless strength of mind is essential when you have planted some hideous thing you lack the courage to demolish. But there is a point when your steadying hand should be lifted, and a bit of native vitality be allowed to take over.

Likewise, the garden of my soul must sometimes be weeded ruthlessly. But there are also times when my "steadying hand should be lifted," times when I should just relax and let what God has planted grow without hovering over it.

We live in such a "doing" culture that we think busyness, especially being busy with things like Bible study, is next to godliness. We mistakenly believe, as my student did, that if we read through the Bible, we will know its truth right away. We forget about a key part of planting: time and space.

An Uncrowded Garden

Gardening can't be hurried. I think part of the current popularity of gardening comes because it stands in sharp contrast to our instant gratification culture. We have cell phones so we can call from anywhere, because we can't wait until we get home or to the office to make a phone call. We send e-mail, or even instant messages, instead of letters. We heat up food in microwave ovens, or just pick up carry-out on the way home from work because even the microwave takes too long.

Our most valuable commodity is not money, but time. The lovely irony about gardening is that it takes a lot of time, and yet, it gives us time: time that is luxuriously unhurried. Even if we buy mature plants instead of seeds, we still can't make them grow any faster than their God-appointed pace. An apple seed will become an apple tree and ultimately produce more apples, but it takes more than a week or two.

Likewise, whatever God is growing in my soul's garden will not crop up overnight. The seed of his Word needs time to germinate and grow. We need, as Jesus said, to retain his Word, to hold it in our heart, to slowly ruminate on it. Rushing is futile. Remember the old bumper sticker slogan: "Be patient, God is not finished with me yet." Transformation takes time.

I know all this is true, but I am often impatient with myself, disappointed with my failures and wanting to see instant maturity, more spiritual fruit. While it's good to desire fruitfulness, I think sometimes I need to cut myself some slack, let go of some perfectionism and just trust that God's timing is perfect. My spiritual journey has been full of backward steps and detours, interspersed with times where I've run full speed ahead. This is as it should be.

Besides needing lots of time, seeds or plants need proper spacing if they are to grow properly. Almost any seed packet will include directions on how far apart to space the plants.

When I plant seeds in my garden, I don't dump the whole

packet into one spot. I spread them out, spacing them so that each has room to grow. Often, once seeds sprout, you have to thin out the plants, pulling up seedlings that are too close together.

One little seed can produce a lot of fruit if it has space and time to grow. It won't produce fruit overnight. If you have too many seedlings together in too little space, they'll choke each other out and none will thrive. Likewise, the seed of God's Word needs uncrowded space in our heart. The Bible is a living document and we interact with it differently at different times in our lives. If we are paying attention when we read it and letting it germinate within the soil of our soul, fruit will develop over time.

Retaining God's Word

In the parable of Luke 8 Jesus said that growth occurs when we not only hear the Word but also "retain" it. How do I hang on to God's Word? Why would I want to?

"I have hidden your word in my heart," the psalmist declares (Psalm 119:11). The reason for having God's Word in our heart, according to this verse, is so "that I might not sin against you."

The impetus behind planting God's Word in my heart and have it sink deep, healthy roots, is to help me live  differently. Retaining God's Word can result in spiritual transformation. Memorizing Scripture can affect the fruitfulness of the garden of my soul.

When I was a child, one pillar of my church's well-constructed Sunday school program was Bible memorization. By the time I was seven or eight years old, I could recite plenty of verses, as

well as all the books of the Bible and numerous facts about biblical characters. We had Bible drills to see who could look up
verses the fastest or recite the most verses. In summer I went to
a Christian camp where we earned badges for memorizing. If
you had a similar background, you may be grateful, as I am, for
a strong foundation for your faith. Of course, you may also
have some dysfunctional messages going through your brain
about memorizing.

So take another look at that second half of the verse in Psalm
119.

It's not "I have hidden your word in my heart that I might
impress you, God."

It's not "I have hidden your word in my heart that I might
get gold stars on my Sunday school chart."

It's not "I have hidden your word in my heart so that I can
quote it, often inappropriately, as a way to manipulate others or
make them think I am a spiritual giant."

The verse says, in essence, that memorizing Scripture makes
it easier to avoid sin. That is, it makes it easier to abide, to live
as Jesus would.

The fact is, it is easier to apply Scripture to your life when it's
stored in your memory, not your bookshelf. It's easier to make
good choices when you are armed with truth. It's easier to
know "What would Jesus do?" if you are at least a little familiar with what he actually did.

If you didn't memorize anything besides the Pledge of Alle-
giance as a child, you may feel intimidated by the idea of memorizing Scripture. But just as you can't plant poppies and
tomatoes at the same time of year, of course you can't memorize
the entire Bible in one sitting. Choose one verse or even a
phrase that is significant or meaningful to you, one that you

read or heard a message on and said "aha!" Then read and say that verse every day for a week or two or three. There's no rush. Write it on a colorful index card and tape it on your bathroom mirror. Pray the verse as you brush your teeth. Soon you'll discover it has become firmly planted in the garden of your soul.

Retention of God's Word is also about obeying it. If you can recite "Love your neighbor as yourself" but have an unchecked gossip habit, you haven't retained God's Word at all. As one of the verses I memorized as a child says, "Be ye doers of the word, and not hearers only, deceiving your own selves" (James 1:22 KJV).

Perseverance

As Jesus continues his explanation of the seed parable, he says that it is our perseverance that produces a good crop, a hundred times what has been sown.

Perseverance is about staying the course, keeping at it for the long haul. But it is not about passively "hanging in there," waiting for a trial to be over.

Often we must persevere through difficulty or trials, in an active, almost aggressive way. We must struggle not only against whatever trial comes our way, but we must also actively fight our desire to just lie down and give up. We don't know the outcome, and we may not know it until we get further along. Perseverance means I have to figure out my next step and then take it. What one thing can I do to persevere, to keep going?

Don't try to plan the entire journey. Just figure out what the next step is. Do the one thing you know you can. It might be small: I can make it to work, I can at least show up. I can listen to a friend or a child, even if I can't give them any help or advice. I can get out of bed. I can set the box of cereal on the table. I can write one good sentence and then, maybe, one more.

James writes that we have an opportunity to develop perseverance when struggles come our way. "Consider it pure joy, my brothers, whenever you face trials of many kinds, because you know that the testing of your faith develops perseverance" (James 1:2-3).

If I truly desire to build this perseverance that Jesus says will result in spiritual fruitfulness, I will be able to see the joy in trials. James goes on to say, "Perseverance must finish its work so that you may be mature and complete, not lacking anything" (James 1:4).

I want to be "not lacking anything," but I don't always want to let perseverance finish its work. I want to persevere for just a little while, which is a contradiction, of course. Instead, I need "a long obedience in the same direction," as Eugene Peterson writes.

Perseverance develops the fruit of patience in my soul. Even if I am not facing a trial, God calls me to persevere in my faith, in cultivating my spiritual life. To keep showing up, letting the Master Gardener in, letting him work and working with him to slowly create something beautiful, something that looks like truth.

If I am an impatient gardener, I could go out and buy plants in containers from a garden center in June and simply set the pots along the front walk. If I keep them watered, I'll have a garden of sorts. But will I know the wonder of the seed?

"A seed has all the potential for life, but as a seed, it is dead," writes Joyce Sackett. "Nothing is happening inside that hard little kernel. No cells are multiplying. But everything is in place inside that seed to produce something greater than the seed itself. When conditions are suitable and the seed's outer coat absorbs enough moisture to allow the inside kernel to swell, the seed comes to life and bursts out of its coat."

One spring my son and I filled an empty egg carton with potting soil and poked a flower seed into each compartment of the egg carton. Using a spray bottle, we soaked the soil each day, keeping it moist but not flooded. A week later tiny seedlings pushed up through the soil. Each morning they had grown taller, awakened by the water, pulled by the magical magnet of warmth, moisture, and eventually, light. And while we had to wait, we also had to do our part by keeping up with the watering. If we neglected that part even for a day, the seedlings would dry up and keel over. The one thing we could do, we had to do, was not hard. We had to water our seeds. We had to persevere and wait patiently for the seeds to grow.

"Patience is not a waiting passivity until someone else does something. Patience asks us to live the moment to the fullest, to be completely present to the moment, to taste the here and now, to be where we are," writes Henri Nouwen.

Gardening demands patience and perseverance. Perennials, plants that come back to life every year, take about three years to establish. The first year you plant them, they may not even bloom, but their roots will grow deep, and they will establish stems and leaves. The plant actually needs time to adjust to the environment in your garden. The second year, they'll bloom lightly, but continue to strengthen their root systems and grow taller. By the third year, if the soil and light in the garden are right, most perennials bloom lavishly.

If the soil and light are not right for that particular plant, it's not going to do well no matter how long I persevere. If I plant something that needs shade, like astilbe, in a corner of the yard that gets strong direct sunlight all day, it's not going to thrive. If I plant tomatoes in a damp, deeply shaded area, I'm going to have to supplement my salads at the grocery store, because tomatoes need sun and well-drained soil to be productive. Helping plants thrive depends on knowing the ideal conditions for that plant.

Likewise, getting things blooming in your soul's garden will depend on understanding yourself and how God created you. Does your soul thrive on contemplative solitude? Or are you the type of person who feels the presence of God in a life of active, fully engaged service or ministry? Are you an extrovert or an introvert, a thinker or a feeler? What feeds your soul?

A full garden may take years to establish as a gardener adds and removes plants in an effort to achieve the result she wants. When I look at a gardening magazine, I find myself wishing I could have the lush and colorful gardens featured on its pages. And I want it instantly, without the hard work.

Likewise, when I read God's Word, I want to be wise and spiritually deep and bear all kinds of spiritual fruit, but I wish I could skip over all the time and effort it takes to arrange my life in such a way that growth will result.

But if I persevere, if I keep at it, being intentional about planting God's truth in the garden of my soul, working the soil and finding ways to practice applying his truth to my daily life, the fruit of patience will slowly develop, even if I am not thinking about being patient. The fruit of the Spirit is a by-product of living intentionally, of living in a way that creates the right conditions for growth.

Perseverance is extremely counter-cultural. In our society, loyalty is no longer valued. Don't like your job? Quit and find another. Marriage getting difficult? File for divorce. Worship services not up to par at your church? Shop around, transfer your membership.

A friend of mine told a story of her preschool son dawdling along as she tried to carry groceries from the car to the house. "Do you think you could go any slower?" she asked in exasperation. "Okay, Mommy," he said, oblivious to her sarcasm, and stopped to study a crack in the sidewalk. She realized that impatience is a form of selfishness: thinking our agenda is more important than anything else.

As I persevere in walking with Jesus, just taking whatever my next step is, I begin to be a little less hectic, less hurried. When that happens, the tiny seedlings of patience begin to grow.

Looking for Seedlings of Spiritual Fruit

When I allow the Master Gardener to plant the truth of his Word in the garden of my soul, I need to keep looking for signs that those seeds are sprouting. I am not merely reading the Bible because it is interesting; I want to be transformed by it. I am finding that the first step in transformation is truly expecting and believing that it can happen.

When I read about God's faithfulness to me, I ask him to help my faith grow. When I learn about the radical love he has for me, I pray he'll help me to love like he did. When I feel afraid, I am comforted by the peace that passes understanding, I know that the fruit of his Spirit is starting to grow in the garden of my soul.

And when I see a little seedling of goodness or faith, when I take a step to be kind instead of cruel, I say, "Look what's coming up in the garden of my soul!" This is not a complete surprise. After all, it's the Master Gardener who is at work in this garden. Still, I need to work with him. I need to ask myself, how can I nurture these seedlings so that they will thrive?

Once a seedling sprouts, it needs regular watering. I have found that planting the seed of God's Word is only the beginning. To grow and mature, I need to let the truth of God's Word soak in so that my roots are strengthened and nourished. Immersing myself in Scripture, I find that my desire for God is quenched and yet quickened. The more I have of him, the more I want.

When I invite the Master Gardener into the garden of my soul, I find that spending time with him in prayer, reflection and meditation allows him to soak his truth deep into the soil. It is to these disciplines that we now turn our attention.

Digging deeper

1. Do you believe God can speak directly to your situation through his Word in the Bible? What is your current approach to reading the Bible?

2. What has been your experience with memorizing Scripture? Do you feel drawn to this spiritual discipline? Select a verse and memorize it.

3. Jesus calls us to perseverance. What barriers keep you from persevering in obedience to him?

6

Water

Transforming Your Heart
Through Reflective Reading,
Prayer and Meditation

The Lord will guide you always;
he will satisfy your needs in a sun-scorched land
and will strengthen your frame.
You will be like a well-watered garden,
like a spring whose waters never fail.
Isaiah 58:11

*I*t is raining. Again. Our little corner of the Midwest is suffering an identity crisis. It thinks it's a rain forest.

A rainier-than-usual spring means more time indoors, at least for my kids, who are getting really good at jigsaw puzzles . . . but beginning to get a bit restless. One blustery rainy day my son stood at the window, shook his fist and yelled at the sky, "No more winter! I want summer!"

But on warmer rainy days in late spring, we don raincoats and venture out to splash in puddles and to work in the garden. Overcast drizzly days are great for planting. Young plants or seeds get a gentle sprinkling through the day, and the sun and wind are subdued enough that they do not dry out the soil. A warm rainy day is a friendly day for new plantings.

The moist spring weather has made my lawn and garden incredibly lush. Anytime the sun comes out, we rush out, happy to see the sun and ready to play. We realize in dismay that anytime it stops raining, we must mow the lawn, which threatens to grow into a forest overnight.

Not surprisingly, a rainy season nurtures growth in my garden. And frequent rain is much more effective than my occasional, impatient visits with the watering can or garden hose.

Looking at the rapid growth of the lawn, the weeds, the lettuce and the peas, I long for lush growth in my spirit, and wonder: how do I water the garden of my soul? That's my desire for my spiritual life: to be growing and alive, like a well-watered garden.

Water imagery springs up throughout the Bible. Jesus referred to himself and to the Spirit as "living water." Longing for God is often illustrated with a metaphor of thirst, while God rains blessings on those he loves. Often a person blessed by God is likened to a tree planted next to a stream: a tree with a readily available supply of life-giving water. "Blessed is the man who trusts in the LORD, whose confidence is in him," the prophet Jeremiah writes (echoing some images from Psalm 1). "He will be like a tree planted by the water that sends out its roots by the stream. It does not fear when heat comes; its leaves are always green. It has no worries in a year of drought and never fails to bear fruit" (Jeremiah 17:7-8).

That's the kind of spiritual life I want: like a tree next to a stream of fresh water. Its roots can slurp up whatever it needs, slowly and constantly. Yet I often feel spiritually dehydrated and wonder, how do I get planted by the river so that I can live a fruitful life?

Blessing, spiritual fruitfulness, is the result of a process. God initiates, asks me to obey. When I do, he shows me how trustworthy he is. Seeing this, I am willing to take another step.

Jeremiah says blessing comes from trusting God, from having confidence in him. To trust God implies that I don't put all of my trust in myself. "Trust in the LORD with all your heart, and lean not on your own understanding" (Proverbs 3:5). Often when I am trying to cultivate my spiritual life, I lean on my own understanding, my own efforts. This, despite my good intentions, is really about a lack of trust.

God has a promise, a blessing, for those who trust him. "In all your ways acknowledge him, and he will make your paths straight" (Proverbs 3:6). The beginning of trust is simply acknowledgment, saying, "Yes, you are," to the one who says, "I AM." When we acknowledge God, he blesses us with his guidance—his making straight paths for us. But sometimes I don't want to take the straight path. I want to go my own way. I want a blessing, but on my terms.

Blessing is not about winning the lottery or getting everything you want. It's about being freed up to fulfill God's purpose for you, trusting that he will help you. It's being satisfied with God.

The more I know about someone, the more I know whether or not I can trust him. So to trust God, I have to get to know him. Ultimately I have to take risks, however small, to see what happens.

I trust certain friends, have confidence in them, when I have known them long enough to see that they are trustworthy. They've got to earn my trust, to come through for me in a tough situation. But they can't earn my trust until I am willing to take a risk, to test and see if they let me down or not.

Larry Crabb writes about how we often try to protect ourselves from rejection by not trusting God or other people. He draws a great word picture of a person standing on a "cliff of safety," connected to God by a "rope of love." As long as we are standing on solid ground (not taking any relational risks), the rope is slack and we don't really know whether it is strong enough to hold us. In order to really know the security of Christ's love, we must jump from the cliff of safety, trusting that the rope of love can indeed support us. When we jump, God promises, his love will catch us, and he will bless us. But the only way to really know that his promise is true is to jump. Not blindly, but in obedience to God.

God's blessing comes to those who trust God, who obey him. But how do we discern what God wants us to do? The Bible says that obedience flows out of delighting in God's law, his Word.

So I come ultimately to this: the beginning of trusting God is knowing him. And the way of knowing him is by meditating on his Word. If I want the garden of my soul to be lush and flourishing, I've got to get the water of the Word flowing through it.

A Gentle Rain

Even the most inexperienced gardener knows that dumping a bucket of water on the garden once or twice a week is not as beneficial as a gentle sprinkling every day or so.

If I water the garden with a bucket, especially if I do it infrequently, most of the water will run off rather than soak in. Delicate seedlings will be drowned and the deep roots of larger plants will never get water because most of it will simply wash away, along with some of the topsoil. If we have a dry spell, I could take the hose and squirt the garden, and soon it will seem that the ground is wet. But if I hoe or shovel the ground, I'll find dust beneath the muddied surface.

The best type of watering a garden can get is a gentle, steady rain that occurs frequently. If I want to approximate that type of watering, I use a soaker hose, a flat hose with tiny holes in it. The hose is laid on the ground along the flower border or between rows in the vegetable garden and allowed to run slowly for quite a while. I water the garden at least every other day unless there is rain. This allows the water to soak gently into the soil, to reach the roots of the plants, not just the surface.

One June I went away for two weeks, taking the kids and leaving Scot at home, since summer is his busiest season at work. "Please water my plants," I told him. I should have been more specific. He watered some, but not all. He watered occasionally, but not very much. Unfortunately we had very little rain during those two weeks.

The pansies were gasping, almost dried up. The lettuces in the window boxes were shadows of their former selves. The rosemary, in a deep pot, had somehow survived, but the thyme in the shallow pot next to it had completely dried out. It was brown, and it crumbled when I touched it.

You could tell the gardener had been away.

Often we try to water the garden of our souls with a quick squirt or a splash of the bucket, rather than a gentle sprinkling. We skim through our assigned Scripture reading for the day, assuaging our guilt but being otherwise unchanged spiritually. Or we may read a lot, gathering bucket loads of information, but it doesn't soak in. Sometimes we get inundated with Scripture or instruction at church and figure that's enough for the week. We equate breadth of knowledge about God with depth of intimacy with him. Either way, my soul remains dry and not much growth results. Even overwatering hurts plants. Avoid overwatering and a plant will sink its tap root deep into the soil in search of moisture and nutrients. Ultimately this strengthens the plant.

So often my spiritual life feels like that thyme plant: dry and crumbly, no longer growing. Or it feels weak and shallow. Often it's because I have not watered the garden properly. I have not taken the time to read slowly and thoughtfully, to reflect and meditate. Or I have flooded my mind with more than it can absorb at one time. I need to pay attention to the ways that I water the garden of my soul.

God's Time Frame

In our effort to grow, sometimes we try to rush things. For much of my life I thought the object of Bible reading was to get it done. I think I'm not alone in this. Many of us don't read the Bible expecting to change. We expect, at best, to gain some information; at least, to get through the reading. The emphasis seems to be on quantity of verses consumed in the shortest amount of time. But what would happen in the garden of my soul if I reversed the equation: a longer amount of time and a smaller quantity of words? Meditation, at its heart, is simply letting the words of Scripture soak in, slowly, as if they were trickling through a soaker hose.

"It is important to resist the temptation to pass over many passages superficially. Our rushing reflects our internal state and our internal state is what needs to be transformed," writes Richard Foster. While reading through the whole Bible is a noble and worthwhile endeavor, I think the pressure to do so within a set time frame can mess with God's planting schedule.

Meditation engages our imagination and creativity. If, for example, I am meditating on the passage where Peter walks on water (Matthew 14:22-32), I may imagine myself in Peter's rather wet shoes. How do I feel as I swing my leg over the edge of the boat, as it pitches on the waves? Is there a lump in my throat when Jesus looks at me and says, "Come"? Or perhaps I imagine myself as Matthew, who watches carefully enough to later record the story of the whole incident, but sits cowering in the boat as that crazy Peter climbs out and walks on water, then starts to sink. Do I wish I had his courage, or merely think him a fool?

When we engage our imagination, we bring more of ourselves to Scripture. Through meditation, we realize that a truth does not have to be rational or intellectually explainable to be true.

You may be put off by the word *meditation*. The idea of meditation is very popular in our "self-help spirituality" culture. It is possible to meditate on anything and not necessarily God. For this reason many Christians think of meditation as an exclusively New Age or Eastern religion practice and therefore miss out on a spiritual experience that can make God more real to them.

Jeremiah's picture of the tree by the water, or the garden with a soaker hose, is a picture of meditation. To take a verse, a thought or idea, and let it soak in slowly. John Ortberg writes:

> Meditation is as slow as the process by which roots draw moisture from the flowing river to bring nurture and fruitfulness to a great tree. Meditation is important enough to be mentioned more than fifty times in the Old Testament. It means not only to think about God's Word, but to read it aloud. Reading the Scriptures out loud gives the reader focused attention and the advantage of learning by both eye and ear. Meditation is likened in Scripture to a young lion growling over its prey, or the low murmur of a dove, or a cow chewing its cud.
>
> Meditation is not meant to be esoteric or spooky or reserved for gurus reciting mantras in the lotus position. It merely implies sustained attention. It is built around this simple principle: *"What the mind repeats, it retains."*

In meditation, subtle nuances are explored, mulled over. The question fueling our quest when we meditate on God's Word is not "What's in it for me?" that is, what knowledge can I gain, what gold stars can I earn for getting my Scripture reading "done"? Rather, meditation bids us ask, "What's it for in me?" In other words, what's the purpose? What change (if I'm open to it) is God's Word going to produce in my life? How will the Word transform my heart?

When we read reflectively or meditate on Scripture, we're not reading for information but rather for transformation. We're letting go of our own timetable, or one imposed on us through our "verse of the day" calendar or our "read through the Bible in a year" schedule, and allowing God to slowly water the garden of our souls.

Soaking the Soil

In recent years I have learned about the value of reading the Bible in a more reflective way. To soak the soil of my soul with God's truth and let the significance of one phrase or even one word penetrate to the roots.

The ancient practice of meditating on Scripture focuses more on what God is saying to me through his Word than what general theological truth a certain passage contains. When I read in this way, reflectively, I look for a word or two that stands out and then I get curious about why that word is important to me. My goal is to slow down and let God touch my heart, rather than just my mind.

Last year I read the book of Ephesians. I started out reading it a section at a time, using the subheads provided in my Bible to tell me when to stop reading, which is how I'd always done it. After a few days I had finished the first chapter. I understood the basics of what I'd read, but I wasn't sure what it had to do with me specifically. I knew from previous studies that

Christians are adopted into God's family. I knew this text has been the source of arguments among Christians about predestination and other issues. But my reading didn't soak down from my head to my heart. My reading didn't result in any change in my heart or in my thinking, and certainly not in my actions.

It's not that I couldn't understand the words. On an intellectual level, the text was quite familiar, perhaps even too much so. I've taught small groups through this book; I've read and studied it numerous times before. But this time it was like I was pouring a bucket of water on the garden of my soul and it was just running off the surface.

So I decided to read it reflectively, as a number of books I'd been reading on spiritual formation suggested. I wanted to try a more meditative approach and allow the Holy Spirit, who had inspired the apostle Paul to write, to stir my heart as I read. I decided that each day I would read just a verse or two and ask God what he wanted to say to me through it. If I needed to, if I sensed God speaking to me through a particular passage, I would stick with it and pray through it for as long as I needed. Reading Ephesians this way took me nearly a year. I'm pretty sure that's how long God wanted me to take.

Sometimes I would copy a verse on an index card and meditate on it for a few days. When I say "meditate," I mean I would tape the index card over the sink and read it every time I was in the kitchen. Or I'd tuck the card in my purse and pull it out any time I found myself with a minute or two: in the car, in a waiting room or while I was waiting for the coffee to brew and the frozen waffles to pop out of the toaster.

If a verse struck me, I often found it helpful to look it up in other translations, especially those that put the Bible into everyday language.

This method of reading has transformed my heart. Having been a Christian for thirty years and having studied at a Christian college, I have a lot of knowledge about the Bible. I have had many seasons in my life where I felt "been there, read that" about reading the Bible. But reading in this more meditative way rekindled my love for God and also my love for Scripture. What an amazing gift the Bible is! I found it to be "living and active," not just an old book of religion that I "ought" to read out of obligation or guilt.

When I told other people about my adventure in Ephesians, I got some interesting responses, especially from those who've bought into the "more and faster is better" theory of Bible reading. They didn't say it out loud, but I think some people wondered if perhaps I was a bit slow, that I just didn't "get it." They were used to approaching the Bible from an intellectual and informational point of view and thought I was doing it wrong.

Still others seemed intrigued, almost to envy me. "A whole year on one book," murmured one, as if I had allowed myself a scandalous luxury.

It's not that I am loafing through Scripture. Really. It's not that I am anti-intellectual. I love to study the Bible, but reflection and study are two different disciplines. Because of the emphasis in my background on more intellectual study, it takes a kind of courage for me to read this way, to do things differently, to let go of all the "shoulds and oughts" in my brain. It also allows what I am reading to soak in, to go deeper than the surface. That, too, takes courage.

As I read through Paul's letter to the church at Ephesus, I kept in mind that this was also God's letter to me. That fact alone, if you stop to think about it, is mind-blowing. And in his letter God had a lot to say to encourage me: he has chosen me, adopted me, forgiven me, loves me. He also had some challenges for me.

One morning I read: "For he himself is our peace, who has made the two one and has destroyed the barrier, the dividing wall of hostility" (Ephesians 2:14). I knew from the context and my reading that the verse was talking about the Jews and Gentiles, that those previously far from God had been adopted into his family. But I wasn't reading for theological meaning or trying to focus on historical context. And while it is important not to take the verse out of context and assign it a new meaning, I was trying to pay attention to what God was saying to me in my unique situation. I was looking for direction and application, promises not just to the Gentiles, but to me, Keri, an adopted child of God.

This particular verse about Christ destroying walls hit me hard, with more than just theological truth. It spoke to me on another level, and that level brought tears. I wasn't sure why at first, but I sincerely believe that Frederick Buechner is correct in saying that "whenever you find tears in your eyes, especially unexpected tears, it is well to pay the closest attention." So I tried to pay attention, although it seemed a bit scary.

"What are these tears about, God?" I asked. And I waited. I knew that God desired unity among his people, and I sensed him nudging me, letting me know that I had put up barriers in my life. I asked him to show me (gently, if possible) what kind of barriers were in it. And as I sat quietly and reflected, and let a gentle rain of God's truth fall, I became aware that there was a "dividing wall of hostility" in my life. Whether out of anger or self-protection, I'd sealed myself off from authentic community with someone I deeply cared about. I often was able to avoid conflict, at least publicly, so I could pretend that everything was fine, but it really wasn't.

As I asked God to help me see things from his perspective, I realized that ignoring the wall of hostility didn't seem to be making it go away. Part of me wanted it down, but another part wanted to just leave it there, or perhaps have it reinforced and tuck-pointed. I was afraid to let Christ knock down the wall, because although it isolated me, it also protected me from pain.

The next day I tried to skim ahead in the text, but God gently pulled me back. So I looked it up in other translations. One version said, "The Messiah has made things up between us so that we're now together on this. . . . He tore down the wall we used to keep each other at a distance."

For a couple of weeks I read that verse again and again, and I prayed, "I don't know how you're going to do it, Jesus, but you say you can destroy the barriers." As I prayed that verse, I became aware of steps he was urging me to take to allow him to break down the wall.

When things get hard and I want to give up, I go back to that verse to remind myself that I'm not on my own when it comes to tearing down the wall. Christ has promised to do that. He has said he will bring peace, because he is peace. As the wall comes down, bit by bit, I get to see some of that peace and it gives me hope.

A Gardening Notebook

Just as my garden benefits from slow and steady watering, my soul will be fed by quiet, unhurried prayer and meditation on God's Word. "Pray without ceasing," the apostle Paul wrote to the early church, knowing that prayer is as necessary to spiritual growth as water is to physical growth.

Unfortunately many Christians wrestle with uncertainty and guilt about their prayer lives. They feel like Paul's directive is an irksome burden, a difficult if not impossible imperative. I, too, have struggled with prayer, but along the way have discovered the nourishing, life-giving power of contemplative prayer.

I love to pray. I'm amazed that God hears me when I think or speak. And beyond that, if I'm not sure how to pray, the Holy Spirit prays on my behalf (Romans 8:26-27). In spite of this I usually have trouble sustaining concentration during my prayers. My mind wanders. For many people, including me, the *idea* of prayer is much more palatable than prayer itself. Knowing my own weakness in this area, I have been journaling my prayers since I was a teenager. This enables me to concentrate, to be specific, and to be able to look back and see what God is digging up in my soul.

Avid gardeners keep gardening notebooks or journals. They note which plants they've grown in which beds. They take notes on the progress of seedlings, the effect of shade on certain plants. They make drawings and other notes to remind them what they planted where and what each plant looks like. They make lists of everything: plants they'd like to try, ones they have tried that didn't work, all kinds of landscaping possibilities. The journals help them to remember what has worked and what has not. It's a way of organizing thoughts and learning from mistakes.

"If you get fed up with your garden looking like a junkyard, get out your notebook," writes gardening expert Sydney Eddison. "It should be cheap and sturdy enough to hold up if it gets damp. Note taking will clear your head and help you establish garden priorities. Make your notes copious, detailed and as specific as possible. Sometimes, the solution presents itself when you identify the problem."

If the garden of your soul feels like a junkyard, get yourself a prayer notebook. It needn't be anything fancy; in fact, it helps to have something small but sturdy that you can keep in your purse or diaper bag or whatever you carry around with you.

Many of my early journals look like a collection of rather formal letters to God, in which I followed a prayer format (Adoration, Confession, Thanksgiving, Supplication). While this was helpful to some degree, it was quite basic and it didn't take into account the landscape of my own soul.

These days my prayer journal looks more like a gardening notebook. Taking notes on my spiritual life often helps me clear my head and establish priorities, just as Eddison's garden journal does. As I write specifically about problems before me, just letting my mind sort through them as I write, I often find God shows me where I can make some changes.

In my journal I often use mind-mapping, with lines and circles and even drawings, to try to discern God's will on a particular topic. I sometimes write in different colors or on a slant, or divide the page into triangles and write about different things in each one.

My journal includes lists of topics for chapters or columns I want to write and people I want to pray for. I write about certain spiritual practices I've tried and whether they seemed to work or not. I even sketch pictures sometimes, knowing that no one else will see it.

When I notice some fruit growing in my life, have an insight or make a good choice, I jot it down. When I notice a weed, I write about it—like last week, when I did something very selfish. I was faced with a choice, to put myself first or to be unselfish. Sadly I didn't even consider the other person's feelings, but only what I wanted.

So I wrote it down. I felt sad, disappointed with myself, deeply convicted. I wrote about that. Then I asked God's forgiveness. I wrote the words, "I'm so sorry." Then I wrote down Psalm 103:12, "As far as the east is from the west, so far has he removed our transgressions from us."

I still feel badly about what I did, but writing down bad choices I make and then taking notes about God's response of grace and forgiveness motivates me not to make similar choices in the future. I'm educated by my journal, just as gardeners learn from their notebooks.

When I'm angry about something or frustrated that things aren't going how I'd hoped, I write horrible, hostile words that no one but God and I can see. I spill my feelings onto the page, write a detailed letter about how I think he ought to run the universe. Sometimes I write things I'd want to spew in anger at a friend or my husband. Once they're out on the page, I can make more rational decisions about confrontation. I can also look at what things might be my fault and listen quietly for what God wants me to do next. Sometimes he only wants me to know that he still loves me. I make sure to take note of that, too.

"Develop the habit of note taking," Eddison advises gardeners. "It requires discipline, but it will pay off. I learned more from my notebooks than from any other single information source, including books, lectures and classes. The notes were often sketchy. There were gaps of months, of a few years, even, but the education of a gardener and the history of an ever-changing garden is all there in these erratic jottings."

You can read books like this one, you can

attend classes on spiritual growth or meditation. These are helpful, but a class or book will not have specific information about *your* particular garden. Just as a gardener's notebook provides an education about one specific garden, a spiritual journal will provide an education about what works and what doesn't, what your priorities are. It will also chronicle the history of God's work in your life, offering you a source of comfort and encouragement when he seems far away.

You may feel intimidated by the idea of journaling, but journaling isn't about crafting perfect prose. It's about taking notes on your life, getting curious about your responses to other people and to God. A journal filled with honest prayers, questions and observations is one of the most crucial tools you can use in cultivating your spiritual life.

Journaling may help me stay focused, but it certainly doesn't guarantee that I will pray with a pure heart. If I'm not careful, my prayers can degenerate into daily mental memos to God, using much the same format as a letter to Santa Claus: "How are you? Hope Mrs. Claus and the elves are doing well. Here's what I'd like for Christmas."

The Bible tells us that if we have needs, we should let God know about them, and God will take care of us (Matthew 6:8 and Philippians 4:19). But that's only one facet of prayer. Before we ask God to solve our problems, we should give him his due in worship and thankfulness. We should be willing to confess our own shortcomings and listen carefully to God about the shortcomings we are blind to.

My prayers often include a list of complaints, things I expect God, or perhaps his celestial customer service department, to fix for me. For example, this morning I wrote a complaint letter in my journal because four families that are our close friends are all moving out of state this month. It seems like every time I get close to someone, build a friendship or take relational risks, God pulls them away from me.

I don't think it's necessarily wrong to let God know about your complaints. Looking at the Psalms, we see that David did more than a little bellyaching, if you ask me, with questions like "Why do the wicked prosper?" and "Why have you forsaken me?" Since David, a man after God's own heart, asked these questions, I think it's okay for me to ask them too. The danger is not in complaining. The danger, for me, lies in telling God how to fix it.

Recently a friend of mine was going through an extremely difficult season. It was definitely winter in the garden of her soul, or perhaps a season of drought. It seemed like almost every aspect of her life was painful and difficult, and things looked as though they would get worse before they got better. As I tried to pray for her, I found myself saying: I don't know what to pray for. I want everything to be fixed, but it's not that easy. I found myself unable to offer God anything to put in his suggestion box except this: Have mercy. Have mercy, please. Do something. I don't know what, but you do.

Sometimes I think that is the most helpful thing to pray, even if we don't know what to say. When we reach the end of ourselves and we realize what has been true all along, that we don't know what's best but God does, all we can say is, "God, please get involved in this situation. Have mercy." And that's enough.

Prayer doesn't have to be formal or long-winded. I think God appreciates simplicity, especially when it reflects our inner state. Writer Anne Lamott says that her two favorite prayers are "Help! Help! Help!" and "Thanks! Thanks! Thanks!"

Even if "Help!" is all you can pray, do it often. If prayer

seems impossible, make a list in your prayer notebook of the reasons why you cannot manage to pray. You may be surprised at what solutions present themselves when you identify the problems.

Like a plant needs water, I need prayer daily. I don't write in my journal every day, but I check in with God each morning before I get out of bed. I spend a couple of minutes giving him the day, asking for his help, thanking him for the grace of another day.

Madeleine L'Engle writes of the lessons learned from an old clock, which had to be wound each day. If it was not, eventually the clock would become useless. "So we must daily keep things wound: that is, we must pray when prayer seems dry as dust; we must write when we are physically tired, when our hearts are heavy, when our bodies are in pain."

In other words, we cannot just pray when we feel like it. If we wait too long between prayers, we may cause considerable damage, especially if our roots are shallow. We need water often, not just when we are feeling "up" spiritually.

God Doing the Seeking

Growing up I memorized Matthew 7:7 from the King James Version, "Ask and it shall be given you; seek and ye shall find; knock, and it shall be opened unto you." That verse and others about persistently seeking God have guided my prayer life. I knew if I wanted to talk to God, I just had to call on his name. The emphasis was on my seeking God and getting other people to find him too. Remember those bright yellow bumper stickers: "I found it"? I had one, even before I had a car.

While it's good to seek after God, I used to think that finding him and connecting with him took the same kind of seeking my kids do when they play hide-and-seek. If I kept looking, maybe I'd find him—but he's tricky, and it would take a lot of work to actually root him out. But the more I read and learned about God, the more I realized something startling: God is not hiding.

Quite the contrary.

In fact, God is the one who is seeking me. He is the initiator. Even when I think things are my idea, it is really he who is prompting my thoughts and desires. Even my desire to pray is God-given.

More than what we say, God is concerned with our attentiveness in prayer. The discipline of silence is a huge part of prayer, yet one I often forget.

For me, the less I say, the more I get out of prayer. Life-changing prayer is not about talking, it's about listening. We may say prayer is communication, but we forget that it should be *two way* communication. In my journal sometimes I write a letter to God, sometimes I try to listen and take notes on what he's telling me.

You may or may not feel that God speaks to you. But how often are you truly silent before him? It's possible that he's speaking, but you're not listening. The discipline of silence and meditation is the beginning of hearing him.

Remember the car radio in your grandfather's car, with the little hash marks and a dial? It had no buttons, no digital tuning. In order to pick up a station, you had to carefully and slowly rotate the dial, listening for the strongest signals. You had to use a gentle touch on the dial, move it slowly back and forth, listening as you turned, until the static cleared and the sound came through clearly. That's how we need to listen to God. Slowly, adjusting as we go, listening intently.

We cannot punch a button and get a digital reading on God.

It takes slow, deliberate listening. Most often he does not speak directly, but simply guides our thoughts, often so subtly that we are not entirely sure whether it is God or us who is generating the thoughts. Part of recognizing the voice of God is learning to stop giving yourself credit for anything profound that comes into your head.

The ongoing conversation, over time, is a deep form of communication with God. Still, communication is only the beginning of prayer. I desire to move beyond simply hearing and being heard, to being with.

When I feel the urge to pray, it is because God wants to talk to me, wants to be with me. "Like the spiritual life itself, prayer is initiated by God," Marjorie Thompson notes.

Realizing that God is the instigator can be very freeing. In part, prayer is simply acknowledging the presence and work of God in my life. As I realized this, I was filled with a hunger to hear God's words. The Bible, especially certain parts of the Old Testament, began to feed me in a new way. My soul was stirred by these words of Hosea: "Let us acknowledge the LORD; let us press on to acknowledge him. As surely as the sun rises, he will appear; he will come to us like the winter rains, like the spring rains that water the earth" (Hosea 6:3).

My desire is to press on to acknowledge God, to realize that he is both the king of creation and the lover of my soul. Acknowledging him means also being aware of my own inadequacies. This awareness does not damage my self-esteem, but instead strengthens it, because while I am insufficient on my own, I am loved and even pursued by a God who is wholly sufficient.

When I catch a glimpse of this truth, it makes

me want to stop treating him like Santa Claus, and instead invite him into the garden of my soul to let his presence rain down on me. When I acknowledge God, he not only gives his presence, but his guidance.

So often I try to manipulate or guide God with my prayers. But really, prayer is about listening, about letting God guide me: not just with answers to my questions, but fulfillment of my longings to be loved and deeply known and encouraged and strengthened.

"I have learned that prayer is not asking for what you think you want but asking to be changed in ways you can't imagine," writes Kathleen Norris. "To be made more grateful, more able to see the good in what you have been given instead of always grieving for what might have been."

"To be made more grateful." I'd like to see that kind of fruit coming up in the garden of my soul.

Abundant Rain

A farmer paces slowly through his fields, checking the plants, which are beginning to look a little withered and dry. His eyes scan the horizon, looking hopefully at the clouds that are beginning pile up. When the skies finally open and pour down a long and steady rain, he stands in his field, arms outstretched, full of joy and relief. Because of God's blessing, his farming efforts will yield a result. That's what I want my prayer life to look like. A rain that will cause the garden of my soul to flower and bear fruit.

In my garden a dry summer is a bit of an annoyance. It means high water bills because I have to run the sprinkler more often. In Bible times no rain often meant famine, as the people were totally dependent on the land for their livelihood and survival. Life revolved around planting, harvesting and whether the rain came "in season."

Throughout the Old Testament there are references to the "spring rains" or the "latter rains." The former rains fell in the late autumn, signaling to the people that it was time to plow and plant seeds. These rains softened the earth and helped seeds to germinate.

The latter rains, or spring rains, fell in late spring and were seen as evidence of God's blessing. The latter rains caused the fruit to ripen, brought the grain to a head, and finished or completed the growth cycle of the plants so that they could be harvested. If God withheld the latter rains, the crops might not mature properly.

Often throughout the Old Testament God withheld rain as a form of judgment. "When the heavens are shut up and there is no rain because your people have sinned against you, and when they pray toward this place and confess your name and turn from their sin because you have afflicted them, then hear from heaven and forgive the sin of your servants, your people Israel. Teach them the right way to live, and send rain on the land you gave your people for an inheritance" (2 Chronicles 6:26-27).

Likewise, he sends rain as a form of blessing: "If you follow my decrees and are careful to obey my commands, I will send you rain in its season, and the ground will yield its crops and the trees of the field their fruit" (Leviticus 26:3-4).

Rain, in that culture, meant life. Today the latter rains are a metaphor for God's grace, for his work in our life that bears spiritual fruit, fruit we could not produce through our own efforts. That grace, that fruit, is something we wait for. It's the focus of our hope. And really that's what prayer is, waiting for God, asking him to act, hoping expectantly that he will. God's

Word is full of promises of abundance, and when we seek him, he will satisfy our thirst for him: "Be glad, O people of Zion, rejoice in the LORD your God, for he has given you the autumn rains in righteousness. He sends you abundant showers, both autumn and spring rains, as before" (Joel 2:23).

I have found that contemplative prayer and reflective spiritual reading have enhanced my ability to abide in Jesus. Interacting with him in this meditative way does not feel like an intimidating burden or an irksome duty, but a way of infusing my spirit with joy and peace. It makes it easier to say yes to the invitation of Christ found in John 7:37-39: "On the last and greatest day of the Feast, Jesus stood and said in a loud voice, 'If anyone is thirsty, let him come to me and drink. Whoever believes in me, as the Scripture has said, streams of living water will flow from within him.' By this he meant the Spirit, whom those who believed in him were later to receive." That Spirit, when it is free to flow, will make the garden of my soul wellwatered.

Digging deeper

1. Marjorie Thompson says, "Spiritual reading is a meditative approach to the written word. It requires *unhurried time* and an open heart. If the purpose of our reading is to be addressed by God, we will need to practice attentive listening and a willingness to respond to what we hear."

What would it take to have unhurried time? What would you have to say "no" or "later" to?

2. How do you typically approach Scripture reading? Try reading reflectively and slowly, going one or two verses at a time. Spend as much time as you need. Journal about your experience: What feelings

did you experience? Did God seem to speak to you through his Word? How willing are you to respond to what God says to you through your reading? What made this easier or harder than a more intellectual approach?

3. When you think of prayer, what comes to mind? Do you feel peace, joy, gentleness? Or maybe guilt and confusion and uncertainty?

Describe a time when you desired God's direction or input. Did you try to listen to him? Did it seem to you that he spoke to you or guided your thoughts?

7

Space

Pruning to
Make Room
for Growth

*The space we give words — whether those words
are the text of Scripture or the texts of our
daily lives — allows them a place to live in our hearts.
Without creating spaces of time in our lives,
we stunt whatever growth the words were meant to produce.*
KEN GIRE

I had been invited to speak to a local church adult Sunday school class. When I arrived, I was surprised to see that the small class was made up of men and women ranging in age from early 30s to mid 80s. I am typically asked to speak for women's groups, typically in a much narrower age range. I wasn't quite sure what I would say to such a diverse crowd. I shot a quick prayer up, asking God to give me the words that the group needed to hear.

We were discussing spiritual growth and how our spiritual life can flourish if we create time and space for God, by slowing down the pace of our lives. One retiree said she wished her life wasn't quite so hurried. I looked at this healthy, silver-haired lady in amazement. She was retired, but felt rushed?

"I have a different activity every day of the week," she said. "Volunteer work, exercise class, things at the senior center. Sometimes it feels like a bit too much. But I think we seniors keep busy because we can see a time coming when we won't be able to do so much, so we want to do it all now." Her class-mates, especially the older ones, nodded sympathetically.

"I understand," I replied. I paused, feeling like God was nudging me to say something else. "But don't you think that when that time comes and you can't do as much, it will be harder to handle than if you haven't had any practice at being still?"

There was a moment of silence that was less than comfortable. For a split second I thought, *Oops!* By the expression on the woman's face, I knew I had struck a chord, and perhaps I had struck it too hard. Sometimes I wonder (as do several of my friends) whether I have a gift of discernment or simply a lack of tact. But I knew I had spoken a truth that the woman, and her classmates, probably needed to hear. I think it was a teachable moment, and God answered my prayer by giving me those words. They were way too true for me to have made them up on my own.

Like many of us, this spry senior had never thought about the fact that if she took some time now to voluntarily be still, she might actually get better at it. She might, if she kept at it, actually learn to be more comfortable with, and even to enjoy, stillness. She might end up better prepared for that time when she won't be able to hop in her car and drive over to the senior center for a game of bridge or an aerobics class.

The woman was quiet, reflecting on the possibility that what I had said might be true. The discussion in the class took an interesting turn. These people had invited me to speak about how to hear God, and I think they were expecting a religious to-do list. But we began to explore the possibility that they might be able to listen to God better if they chucked the long list of religious and civic activities and just got quiet.

Others in the class chimed in with admissions about how they kept busy and how they would feel guilty if they did not. We talked about what God might be up to in their lives, what he might be saying, how keeping busy made it hard to hear his quiet voice.

I'd like to think that God inspired the folks in that class to slow down, to let him cultivate the garden of their souls. Maybe that happened. I don't know. But I do know that God used that incident to do some major work in my soul. After talking with the group about listening and slowing down, I realized that I needed to do those things. I kept thinking my life would eventually slow down, but here was this eighty-year-old who was thinking the same thing. In this woman God showed me a picture of myself and whispered: "Unless you sit still, this will be you at eighty years old. You'll still be trying to do it all and thinking that someday soon things will really settle down."

Hurry doesn't end when you retire. It is possible to hurry for your whole life and never get any closer to where you really want to be.

We live hurried lives. Time flies, whether we are having fun or not. But does it have to? If I allow God to prune my life, slow it down and simplify it, to cut the sinful or destructive patterns out of it, I am likely to grow. I hear many people say that all of life can be spiritual, but this can only begin to be true in my life if I stop rushing past everything. There is a paradox: in doing more, I rush past my life and see less.

If I am trying to cultivate the garden of my soul, but I never stop to enjoy the beauty and wonder of what God is doing in and through my life, what's the point? Joy, a key characteristic of spiritual fruit, grows strong in my life when I see God in it. If I am moving too fast, keeping my life too full, I don't get a chance to experience God in the midst of things. And if I never prune things back, my garden will be less fruitful.

Wayne Jacobsen writes, "If a vine is pruned correctly, its growth will spread out evenly. It will carry the right amount of fruit to term, and its shape will facilitate the care it needs through all of the growing season. What a marvelous picture of the surgery God performs in our lives! He prunes us so we can bear more fruit. He cuts away the clutter from our lives."

My life has a lot of clutter. It's hard for me, but I need to let God come in and direct my pruning efforts. The pruning begins with slowing down, with staking out space and time in my life where I can join God in tending to the garden of my soul. I need to learn to say no to some of the activities that distract and hurry me. Sometimes this means just cutting activities from my schedule in small ways: pruning that is not drastic, but ever so helpful.

Pruning an Ordinary Day

A garden benefits from regular pruning. As flowers finish blooming, they'll bloom again if you "deadhead" them, which sounds frightful but simply means removing the spent blossoms so the plant can focus its energies on growing new flowers. Typically the best way to do this is on a daily basis throughout the flowering season.

When I can prune my life in small ways, I can create pauses in my day—little spaces where God can show up, or sometimes just his peace can pervade.

Today was a busy day, but it did not feel hurried. Yes, there is a difference. Sometimes we have obligations and commitments that keep us busy, but if we fulfill those obligations calmly and gently, we can avoid feeling anxious and hurried. "Busy" is based on what we do, the condition of our daily planner; "hurried" is how we may feel about it, the condition of our heart. Sometimes the difference between hurried and not hurried is some subtle pruning, some careful building in of pauses where we can catch our breath.

Knowing my morning would be a full one, I decided to try and prune those things that were not completely necessary. I wanted to eliminate hurry (that inner anxiety) while still doing what really needed to get done. That is, to distinguish between needs and wants when it came to the use of my time.

After getting my daughter (with her backpack and lunch packed) out the door at 7:45 a.m. for the carpool, I had a little time where my son was playing and I was still in my pajamas. I had a little window of solitude, for about twenty minutes, in my office with the door closed. I spent some time praying, journaling, just sitting quietly.

A little while later my in-laws called: they were in the neighborhood, could they stop by? I made a choice not to scurry around the house picking up, but instead put on a fresh pot of coffee and just enjoyed visiting with them for a little while.

Soon I had to drive my son to music class. While he was in class, I decided not to attempt a mad dash through the nearby grocery store as I sometimes do. There were a few things I wanted to pick up, but I wanted to eliminate hurry. I pictured myself sprinting through the store grabbing things off shelves and knew that I could not avoid hurry if I went to the store. The shopping could wait. Instead, I just spent the thirty minutes in the waiting room at music class. I made lists on my calendar. I chatted with the other moms, just kind of hanging out. I created another little island of mental space in my day.

We got home from music class and had a simple lunch. Then we were off to swimming lessons. While Aaron paddled in the pool, I jogged slowly on the treadmill in the workout room that overlooks the pool. While that may not sound relaxing, it was much more refreshing than my typical *modus operandi*, which involves plugging my laptop into an outlet in the observation area and trying to write while the kids have their lessons.

I had thought about running errands that afternoon, but I decided that since I was trying to eliminate hurry, I would put them off. We could get by another day or two without going to the discount store or the dry cleaners.

Instead, Aaron and I went home. We pulled out brown and orange construction paper and made a turkey, in honor of Thanksgiving, which was the next week. I traced his hand, then together we cut out the shape, then glued orange paper feathers on it. The result didn't resemble a turkey very much, but we didn't care. The joy of guiding his hands in mine as we worked the safety scissors, the look of concentration on his face as he painted a yellow beak on the turkey, and his triumphant smile when we hung the project on the refrigerator door made the process feel much more important than the end result. We staked out a little time to connect as mom and son, not just chauffer and passenger.

Later I folded some laundry and emptied the dishwasher, letting Aaron match the socks and sort the silverware. Throughout the afternoon I felt like God was very close, a quiet, peaceful presence.

Soon my daughter came home from school, bringing two friends over to play while I got dinner started. The house was full of the noise of kids playing and the smell of dinner cooking. Again I felt God's comforting presence. Maybe because of the way I had paced my day. I don't know. I felt peaceful and joyful and connected with God, even as I made a casserole and set the table. If I'd done my day differently, though, would I have noticed his presence? Would it have been as peaceful?

And now the kids are in bed, and I'm writing this chapter. Again, I think if I'd done my day differently, I might be crashed on the sofa, staring blankly at the television. Fortunately I'm not.

It was an ordinary day, really. Yet if I had made some different choices, attempting to fit more in, it could have felt a bit frantic. In the midst of ordinary busyness I did one thing over and over: I *decided* not to hurry. I *decided* not to do certain things. I didn't spend more time in prayer or Bible reading than I normally do. But as I slowed the day, I realized over and over that sometimes what I call "needs" are actually "wants." Sometimes they're not even "wants." They're just an excuse to do something, to keep myself running. That realization has opened a window so that I could see God's provision for me and for my family.

Making decisions to prune my schedule allowed me to create enough space to avoid that inner panic of hurry. I made choices about the things I could, and I *decided* not to worry too much about the things beyond my control. I chose construction paper turkeys over dusting or a run to Target. The dust bunnies lie undisturbed, we're almost out of dish soap, but the garden of my soul is blooming.

Slowing Down in a Fast Culture

For our tenth anniversary Scot and I took a long overdue vacation, minus children. My parents came to stay with the kids, and I wrote down the weekly schedule. "Pick up Melanie from school, bring snacks, take her to piano lessons, don't forget her music bag," the first entry noted.

The next day's outline included these notes, among others:

"Aaron will be picked up at noon for school, probably by Lisa but it might be Jo, then you have to pick him and his friend up from school at 2:45. Janet will call you if her son needs a ride as well. Melanie gets home an hour after that, and needs to have a snack, do her homework and practice piano, and then get to swimming lessons at 5."

Half a week of activities filled two pages of a legal pad, and my mom looked at me incredulously. "How do you keep all this straight?" she asked.

All what straight? I'd never thought the pace of our lives was that crazy. It was normal, although it did seem like a lot when I wrote it down. But our lives are simple compared to a lot of my children's peers. Many of the six-year-olds I know are on two sports teams, plus AWANA club and ceramics and piano, or Brownies, ballet and tae kwon do. I know a lot of kids who have after-school activities each day of the week.

Parents, and by extension their children, are not immune from the hurry sickness that infects our world today. Standing with other moms near the playground, watching the kids play in mid-summer, a typical conversation begins with, "So, what are you signing your kids up for this fall?"

There's a tremendous pressure on parents to enroll their children in sports and other activities at a very young age. We want to make sure our kids don't fall behind or miss opportunities, so we sign them up for screenplay writing class as soon as they learn their ABCs.

We sign up our kids for everything, and then we complain because we are too busy. What's wrong with this picture?

My husband and I enjoy sports. We are not professional athletes, but we've been playing various sports our whole lives. But like most people our age, our athletic endeavors were pretty much limited to tag or kick-the-can until we were nine or ten years old. Real competition didn't happen until high school. I don't think we ended up missing out on opportunities by waiting. Why, then, did I feel compelled to put my son in T-ball when he was four and my daughter in ballet at age three?

Mostly, I think, it was due to peer pressure. It's the same pressure that made me play classical music to my belly when my kids were still within it, and read *Little Women* to Melanie as I nursed her. I wanted to stimulate those brain cells, give my kids every advantage they could possibly get as soon as possible.

It's become a part of our culture to replace play with lessons. Fueled by features on Wide World of Sports, where we see home movies of Tiger Woods and Andre Agassi playing golf and tennis as preschoolers, we can't help but think, *That could be my kid! I've got to get started earlier if he's going to be a star!*

But why do we need our kids to be stars? What if they are simply lovely, kind people who enjoy recreation, but don't end up on center court at Wimbledon? What if they just played and had a childhood until they were old enough to decide for themselves whether they really want to take dance classes or play Little League?

If they have it in them to be a star, will starting earlier help them significantly? What if Tiger Woods had picked up a golf club at age nine instead of two? Would he be a mediocre player today? I doubt it.

Seasonal Pruning

This season, this summer, I am doing some radical pruning of our schedule. I am signing my children up for . . . nothing.

That's right. No swim lessons, no camps, no sports leagues.

After perusing park district catalogs and talking to friends who are trying to figure out how they are going to get three kids to three different lessons in three different places at the same time, I had this radical thought: summer camp is optional. Swimming lessons are optional. School is out for summer, and there is absolutely nowhere that we have to be.

This school year has been busy, with my son in preschool and my daughter in first grade. The spring has been full, with all kinds of school activities, choir concerts, T-ball games, soccer practices and variety shows. I keep thinking, "When am I going to have some time to write, to just slow down and not be carpooling every day? And when are my kids going to have time to just play?"

Then it hit me: I am the only one who can slow down my own life. It will require some drastic action on my part, or perhaps, deliberate lack of action. So I'm watching my friends sign their kids up for art lessons and karate and thinking, *I don't have to do that.* My friends, it seems, are surprised, taken aback by the possibility that we might have a choice in all of this.

"That sounds really great," they respond when they hear about my pruned summer. But they keep on reading two differ-

ent park district catalogs and drawing up schedules. I think they suppose I am crazy, or that my kids will be missing out. I feel like I am giving my kids an extravagant gift: unhurried time.

When my kids' spring sports seasons end (both in mid-June), we are going to have a vacation. First, to see my parents for a couple of weeks. My mom has promised to play with the kids while I write. Then, for the rest of the summer we'll be home, but we are taking a vacation of another kind. A vacation from hurry. From having to be anywhere at any particular time. From driving my kids all over our little universe.

I have the luxury of doing this because I work at home. Parents who work outside of the home have to get creative in summer, with juggling childcare and day camps so their kids will be supervised while they are at work.

It's not going to be a boring summer, though. In addition to the normal day-to-day running of our home and spending time with my kids (who obviously will not be away at camp), I am writing this book. Lest you think I am a martyr or magician, I'm already interviewing my babysitters to see which one wants to spend two mornings a week at my house, playing with my kids while I'm in my office working.

But playing with the sitter in the back yard is different from going to soccer camp. Some may say it sounds boring. Maybe. But I want my kids to taste a long, relaxed summer. If they get bored, I want them to discover that they can read a book, or have a lemonade stand, or dig for worms in the back yard, or play tag, or climb a tree, or lie on the grass and look at the shapes of clouds. I am not going to entertain them, at least not very often. That's not my job.

I want to give them a little taste of the kind of summer that I had as a child. The kind most kids don't have anymore. My children are now five and seven, still young enough to appreciate this. They're still at the stage where being "creative" won't get them into too much trouble. Even when the sitter isn't there, they can play by themselves a bit. Maybe I'll set up the laptop on the deck while they run through the sprinkler in the yard.

Instead of swimming lessons, I'll take them to the pool and swim with them. Instead of art class, I'll bring them out in the yard and have them draw a picture of the garden as I pull weeds. Or not. The freedom of unscheduled time awaits us, to fill with picnics and playing, or simply being.

You may wonder how pruning your schedule will help you to cultivate your spiritual life. Why is it that hurry is the enemy of the spiritual life? If we want God to help us to grow, we've got to create some time and space for him to work. Spiritual growth begins with the nitty-gritty of your daily and weekly schedule. To say yes to God, we sometimes have to say no to other things.

The Art of Saying No

The garden of my soul cannot flourish if it is too crowded. I must do some pruning and digging out, creating some space if I want it to be productive and beautiful. Certain classic spiritual disciplines have helped me in the fine art of saying "no."

Slowing down is the first way I've learned to say no. As I have tried deliberately to slow my life down and spend time in solitude, I've given God a bit of time and space to do some gardening, to show me what I truly need and what I merely want.

Saying no to hurry has shown me the power of refusing. When I refuse to buy into the cultural norms of more stuff, more activities, more work, I find I have excess room in my life. Saying no to certain things has enabled me to say yes to God. Lately I've felt God calling me to greater trust in him, to acknowledge him and his ability to meet my needs. I've been drawn to the ancient discipline of fasting as a way to get even more clarity about this issue of needs and wants.

"Are we aware of how much sustains our life apart from

physical food? Do we have an inner conviction that Christ is our life? We will comprehend little of how we are nourished by Christ until we have emptied ourselves of the kinds of sustenance that keep us content to live at life's surface," writes Marjorie Thompson.

Content to live at life's surface. So often, despite my desire to abide and send my roots deep, this describes me rather accurately. My roots are shallow, in part, because I am afraid of doing what it will take to grow them deeper. But I will never be fully satisfied with God until I give him a chance to be all that satisfies me. By temporarily abstaining from both wants and needs, I learn to trust God and acknowledge that he is all I need.

I used to fast regularly. I would abstain from all food and drinks, except a bit of pure fruit juice and water, for the twenty-four hours preceding my church's mid-week worship service. I wanted to come before God focused on him, emptied of all else so that I could let him fill me up. The problem was, by the end of a busy workday, I would typically get tired and light-headed. One night at church one of our teaching pastors read a story, an allegory of Christ's sufferings, which included some rather vivid bloody imagery. I faint quite easily, especially when there is blood involved. Weakened by not having eaten for more than twenty-four hours, I passed out cold, right in my chair. Scot, who was my boyfriend at the time, was a little freaked out, to put it mildly. That put me off fasting for a while—like for about a decade.

But fasting doesn't necessarily have to mean such severe restrictions. Fasting can be as simple as skipping a meal—not because you are too busy to stop to eat, but instead having the intention of focusing on God. Just making the choice about whether to skip a meal or not should be a sober reminder that many people in the world do not have such choices. They skip meals not to lose weight or to fast, but because food is simply not available.

"A body needs food," wrote former missionary Elisabeth Elliot. "Food is a question of discipline for us who live in very rich, very civilized, very self-indulgent countries. For those who have not the vast array of choices we have, food is a fundamental matter of subsistence and not a major hindrance to holiness. . . . One way to begin to see how vastly indulgent we usually are is to fast."

Food can easily be a "hindrance to holiness." If fasting from all food and drink intimidates you, try fasting from junk food. Or fast from soda or other drinks, drinking only water with your meals. For me even eliminating extras like sweets can be a tough discipline.

Just Say No . . . to Jelly Beans

As much as I want to move toward a more disciplined life, one of my weaknesses is my sweet tooth. Especially jelly beans. So as I tried moving back into the discipline of fasting after my ten-year hiatus, I began with fasting from sweets.

How hard can it be to just skip the sugar? I thought. Ha. It was amazing to discover how often I would search the cupboards for a small smackeral of something, as Winnie the Pooh would say. I'd find myself in the kitchen, opening the pantry, when I'd realize, "Oh yeah, I'm fasting from sweets." So I'm not going to have my mid-morning cookie or my mid-afternoon handful of jelly beans or my late-afternoon chocolate.

The trips to the kitchen reminded me to pray. I'd walk out of the kitchen, go to the living room and pray. And I would listen for a moment to what God was trying to tell me (besides the obvious fact that I'm way too fond of sugar). Typically, in these moments, every word from God was one of reassurance. The verse in Jeremiah that says, "For I know the plans I have for you, plans to give you a hope and a future," chorused through my head, and God would even adapt them to my own situation. When I'd sit still long enough to admit my insecurities to him, then wait, I would feel his gentle reassurance.

I realized that in those moments of craving a sweet, I wasn't really hungry, at least physically. There was this side of me that was restless, pacing like a tiger in a cage, bored and over-whelmed at the same time. I often headed to the kitchen when I was frustrated with the kids, or facing writer's block, or was simply bored.

Sometimes I would snack because I was experiencing not writer's block but mom block. Do you ever have mom block? It's when you're just not sure what you should do next as a mom, and you kind of freeze. You want to resign but you don't have a boss to resign to. You feel tremendous guilt and you wonder how to get unstuck.

Try fasting when you hit a mom block. Fasting doesn't have to involve food. You can fast from certain actions or media. Have you ever tried fasting from that which holds you in its grip? Television. Gossip. Shopping.

Fast from television for a week. Get one of the books I recommend in the back of this book and read it instead of watching television. Fast from junk food. Fast from yelling. Fasting can unblock mom block.

"In a more tangible, visceral way than any other

spiritual discipline, fasting reveals our excessive attachments and the assumptions that lie behind them," writes Marjorie Thompson. "Food is necessary to life, but we have made it more necessary than God. How often have we neglected to remember God's presence when we would never consider neglecting to eat! Fasting brings us face to face with how we put the material world ahead of its spiritual Source."

What Fasting Is Not

Fasting is perhaps the most misunderstood of spiritual disciplines. It's important to realize what fasting is not. It is not a way to bribe God, to manipulate him into granting our every wish, to get him to listen better to our prayers. It is rather a way to get us to "listen better" to what God is telling us. It can be a test of whether what we're praying for really matters as much as we think it does. Elisabeth Elliot writes:

> A friend of mine recounted how she had been hammering away at heaven's door for the answer to a certain prayer. Nothing seemed to be happening. She began to get angry at God because He wasn't doing anything. Then He seemed to say quietly, "Why don't you fast?"
>
> "Then it came over me," she said. "I didn't really *care* that much."

Sometimes eating can be a way of anesthetizing ourselves to the point of spiritual and even mental grogginess, so that we cannot hear the whisper of God. When we fast, hunger pangs remind us to refocus on God, to bring our whole selves, including our physical selves, before him. It wakes us up to our own weakness and God's strength. If it makes us tired or weary, that can be a way of reminding ourselves to depend upon him.

We come up with plenty of ways to avoid fasting. In my case I assumed fasting had to be extreme in order to be effective. I thought I had to go at least twenty-four hours, with nothing but water and perhaps a little fruit juice. Unable to handle that very well, I gave up on a spiritual discipline that can be incredibly transforming.

Yes, it can be transforming. Unfortunately fasting can also cause the weed of pride to sprout up in the garden of my soul. Jesus knew this, which is why he warned us not to let people know when we are fasting (see Matthew 6:16-18).

To keep my ego in check, and my blood sugar at a safe level, I have been experimenting lately with partial fasts. I eat just a bit of bread or fruit, enough to keep me from passing out, but not enough to satisfy me completely. I ask God to make up the difference, to sustain and satisfy me in a way that a crust of bread cannot.

Much of the world subsists on simple food like rice and beans. Connect spiritually with God and with the poor by setting aside a day where you will eat no more than two bowls of beans and rice and drink only water. You'll go to bed a bit hungry, as more than half the people in the world do every night.

Fasting can be a regular discipline, engaged in once a week or once a month, or it can be done to accompany prayer over a particularly pressing concern. Traditionally fasting was done to express repentance or to prepare for a mission (as Jesus did during his forty days in the wilderness).

Isaiah 58 is an excellent chapter to meditate on as you consider fasting. If we deny ourselves food but allow ourselves to rage, this passage warns, God is unmoved. We're wasting our time. "Your fasting ends in quarreling and strife, and in striking each other with wicked fists. You cannot fast as you do today and expect your voice to be heard on high" (v. 4).

The chapter goes on to say that the result of fasting should be softer hearts. Fasting should not only sharpen our hearing for God's words, but it should build our compassion for the poor and inspire us to act on their behalf: "Is not this the kind of fasting I have chosen: to loose the chains of injustice and untie the cords of the yoke, to set the oppressed free and break every yoke? Is it not to share your food with the hungry and provide the poor wanderer with shelter?" (vv. 6-7).

If you decide to make a regular habit of fasting, figure out about how much money you'll save on food. Say, for example, you decide to fast once a week. Determine the cost of the meals you forgo, depending on whether you eat out or at home, and put that much into an envelope on the day you fast. (Don't go spend your lunch money at the Gap!) By the end of the month you will likely have enough to sponsor a hungry child (maybe two!) through World Vision. This can enlarge your heart for the poor and may provide some much-needed motivation as you attempt this spiritual discipline.

God will satisfy those who fast in this way. If we read a bit further in Isaiah 58, we find God's promises: "If you spend yourselves in behalf of the hungry and satisfy the needs of the oppressed, then your light will rise in the darkness, and night will become like the noonday. The LORD will guide you always; he will satisfy your needs in a sun-scorched land and will strengthen your frame" (vv. 10-11).

Finally, one more thing that fasting is not. In our weight-conscious society, fasting may appeal to those trying to lose a few pounds. But fasting is not about earning some spiritual brownie points while you pray your way to a trimmer and slimmer you.

If your motive is weight loss, be honest about it. If your motives are mixed, admit it. If you don't know how to disentangle your motives, try fasting from things other than food, or try eating just enough to sustain yourself, but not satisfy yourself completely. Ask God to satisfy you.

Saying no to certain things isn't easy, especially in today's culture. In a way, disciplines like slowing down or fasting are harder than other ways in which we resist the popular culture of our day. I mean, keeping busy, even overly busy, is not illegal or immoral. It is the same with eating, or even over-eating. Slowing down is an especially hard discipline for parents who don't want to deny their children "opportunities." But if we don't make the small decisions to prune, to pause, things can get out of control. If we ignore the need to prune regularly, whether we're cutting from our schedules or our gardens, pruning eventually becomes a matter of life and death.

Ruthlessly Pruning Branches

In a sunny corner of my back yard stands a small Japanese maple, planted there by the previous owners. One year I noticed it looked a bit sickly. In mid-summer it looked as though autumn had come early to its left side, where its leaves were shriveled and dried out. The tree appeared to be dying. I wasn't sure what to do, so I did nothing—except worry a bit about it and think to myself whenever I walked past it, "I should do something." I guess I hoped it would improve on its own. Instead, the tree got worse.

I asked a landscaper about the tree and said, "I guess I should have it taken out." Not at all, he replied. He told me that the tree was quite valuable and had potential for great beauty, but it needed some surgery.

He told me to prune away all the branches that appeared to be diseased and to spread a thin layer of Vaseline on the wounds left by my pruning saw, to protect the tree. I was dubious about the tree's chances for survival, but he said it would surely die if I did not prune it. So I got out the hacksaw and set to work.

When I got done, the tree looked like an obscene modern art rendition of its former self. Only two main branches remained, both on the right hand side of the tree. These still bore healthy leaves, but the rest of the tree was reduced to lifeless-looking stumps, smeared with petroleum jelly.

Later that season some new baby branches began to sprout from the tree's pruned side. By the next year the tree no longer looked quite so lopsided. By the year after that it was full and healthy, pulled back from the clutches of death by what felt like a severe pruning.

Cutting things out, slowing your life, is extremely counter-cultural. But if you don't take small steps, God may eventually need to do some more drastic pruning. Submitting to God's pruning of sin and bad habits is difficult. And remember: it took my tree several years to recover. Pruning doesn't always yield immediate results.

Then again, the Master Gardener usually isn't interested in the quick fix. He's looking at things from an eternal perspective, and he's very patient, and very gentle. He doesn't just come through the garden with a machete. He prunes very deliberately, and the characteristics he displays as he's pruning—patience, gentleness, self-control—are some of the very things that he's trying to cultivate in us.

Digging deeper

1. Write down your weekly schedule. Include the activities of every person in your household. Is your life hurried? How does this affect your spiritual life? How does it affect your ability to connect as a family? Where could you prune back your involvements to create more space for God?

2. What dead branches crowd your life? Are there unhealthy patterns or habits that God is trying to prune from your life? What is keeping you from allowing him to remove them?

3. Have you ever tried fasting? If so, what happened? What is your response to God's invitation to engage in this spiritual practice?

8

Rest

Establishing a
Sabbath Rhythm

*For me, Sabbath has come to represent
as much a state of mind as a day of the week.
It means time out for the soul, time to lay aside my
daily cares in favor of spiritual refreshment.
It is a way of separating time into different parts
and experiencing it in different ways.
I do not feel that I am losing any time by
spending my Sunday morning in church
and Sunday afternoon with my family.
On the contrary, I am taking time back.*
KATRINA KENISON

*T*he idea of pruning my schedule eventually created in me a desire to slow down not just occasionally, but to slow down the overall pace of my life. It led me to try another discipline, keeping Sabbath. I felt that God was calling me to find a rhythm of life that feeds my soul, allowing for a time of work and a time of rest.

As you slow your life, on an occasional day or an occasional season, you may be drawn to trying to establish a slower pace. You may want to engage in a pattern of life that marches to a more measured, slower beat. You may want to try and open up more space for God on a regular basis.

A Day of Rest

God knows that both people and land need regular rest to be productive and healthy. Just before the children of Israel went into the Promised Land of Canaan, God gave them some instructions for governing themselves and for the use of their land: "For six years sow your fields, and for six years prune your vineyards and gather their crops. But in the seventh year the land is to have a sabbath of rest, a sabbath to the LORD. Do not sow your fields or prune your vineyards" (Leviticus 25:3-4).

The idea of a Sabbath for the land is smart agriculture. Modern farmers often rotate crops to avoid depleting the soil. Letting the land lie fallow for a year allows soil nutrients, which are necessary for healthy plants, to replenish themselves.

In my own garden I build my compost pile in a different spot each year. The spot with the pile is the one that gets a "rest" that year. This spot, with compost decaying on top of it, is usually the most productive part of my garden the following season. This is due in part to the fact that no plants are drawing nutrients out of the soil, and also because of the compost, which adds nutrients to the soil. It's actually a perfect picture of how to create a Sabbath: add things that feed us, avoid things that deplete us.

According to God's Sabbath plan for the land, grain or fruit that sprung up on its own during the Sabbath year could be eaten. Giving the land time to rest and replenish the nutrients in the soil ultimately made it more productive, but the children of Israel may have been a little uncertain, or even voiced some objections about this Sabbath for the land. How would there be enough food? Likewise, when I think about taking a day off, I worry. How will I get everything done if I take time out for rest and reflection?

The Sabbath, for the land or for people, is a call to trust. The Israelites had to truly depend on God for the food that the land provided in that Sabbath year. I have to trust that God will help me accomplish everything I need to do.

God knows us well enough to realize how hard it is for us to obey, even when the commandment is to rest. A few verses after the command for the land's Sabbath, I found this promise: "You may ask, 'What will we eat in the seventh year if we do not plant or harvest our crops?' I will send you such a blessing in the sixth year that the land will yield enough for three years. While you plant during the eighth year, you will eat from the old crop and will continue to eat from it until the harvest of the ninth year comes in" (Leviticus 25:20-22).

God promised that if his children honored his command, he would provide—not just a little, but abundantly. He also warned that if they didn't, they'd be severely punished (Leviticus 26:14-39). Taking a Sabbath can be a way to learn experientially that God will take care of me, and he will even make me more productive the rest of the week, if I can cease striving for one day.

This is not easy. It wasn't easy for the nation of Israel. In fact, despite God's promises, the Israelites violated his commandment. Some scholars believe that their refusal to give the land rest was part (or all) of the reason that the Israelites ended up exiled in Babylon. While they were there, the Bible says, "The land enjoyed its sabbath rests; all the time of its desolation it rested" (2 Chronicles 36:21). In other words, when the people wouldn't give the land a rest, God found a way to make it happen.

Likewise, if we don't obey God's command to rest, we're going to end up burned out and exhausted and get to a point where we'll have no choice but to rest. I don't think God causes this in some sort of punitive way. But if we run too fast for too long, exhaustion is just a natural consequence for our actions.

The How and Why of Sabbath

The Bible commands us to take a day off, to keep the Sabbath holy. Why then don't we obey this commandment? More important, why doesn't this bother us? If I tell a lie or steal something, I feel conviction and guilt. If I violate the Sabbath, do I even notice?

What does it mean to "remember the Sabbath"? Oh, many of us go to church. We can do that "sacred assembly" thing and may even enjoy it, as long as church gets out on time. But giving the whole day to the Lord, setting aside our to-do list for a whole day—that's a little harder. I think there are two reasons we don't practice the discipline of Sabbath: we don't know how and we don't know why.

The film *Chariots of Fire* tells the compelling story of missionary Eric Liddell, who was part of the 1924 Olympic track team for England. The team goes to the Olympic games in Paris, where Liddell's first qualifying heat is scheduled for Sunday. Liddell refuses to run on the Sabbath, despite the efforts of the Olympic committee to convince him otherwise.

"If I win, I win for God," Liddell tells the committee. "Now I find myself sitting here, destroying it all. . . . To run would be against God's law."

Finally a teammate volunteers to trade events with him so that Liddell can run in a different race, the qualifying heat of which will be held on Thursday. After the switch is discussed and decided on, two members of the committee discuss Liddell and his unusual stance. "The lad almost had us beat," says one. "Oh, but he did beat us," replies the other. "And thank God he did. The lad, as you call him, is a true man of principle and a true athlete. His speed is a mere extension of his life, its Force. We sought to sever his running from his Self."

It's an amazing story of a man of strong faith, principles and God-given talent. It's about God honoring a man who chose to honor him, even though it was difficult.

But does that mean that someone like Mike Singletary, former linebacker for the Chicago Bears, and also a committed Christian, was violating the fourth commandment during his entire NFL career? When he played football every Sunday for almost half the year and did the work he was paid to do (and did it very well), was he doing wrong?

Is it wrong for my husband to work on Sundays? He's a realtor, and Sunday is often a busy day when clients want to see homes.

And what about my daughter, who during part of the year has soccer games every Sunday afternoon? If you go to church Sunday morning but play soccer on Sunday afternoon, are you violating the Sabbath? Does it count if you're just playing in the back yard? If I refuse to allow her to compete in soccer games on Sunday, will she grow up resenting God because he didn't allow her to have fun on Sunday? If her daddy works on Sunday, but I don't let her play soccer on Sunday, what am I teaching her besides hypocrisy?

One of my favorite ways to reconnect with my husband is to race our sailboat. It's a two-person boat, and racing requires us to work together. It's physically demanding, but we have a blast. The races are held on the lake where his parents live. On the rare summer weekends that Scot doesn't have to work, we drive up to the lake, skipping church. His mom plays with the kids and we race our sailboat. Eric Liddell might disapprove. And yet to us, it feels like a day of rest and recreation. It refreshes our spirits, rejuvenates us. So are we obeying the Sabbath or violating it?

Rather than try to untangle these legalistic questions, most people give up on even trying to observe the Sabbath. We simply don't know how to do it. We know what it means to live for the weekend, but we don't know how to be intentional with a day of rest.

We also don't know why we observe the Sabbath. In a world of e-commerce and digital communication, workaholism seems to be a mark of success. To keep ahead, or even to keep up, we run at Mach speed 24-7. We work hard all week, then play hard on weekends. We work outside the home during the week, work at home on the weekend (checking e-mail and voicemail, doing paperwork or catching up on housework and grocery shopping). We're afraid if we stop running the rat race for even one day, all the other rats will get ahead of us.

Although many people have Saturday and Sunday off from their regular job, their weekends are full of busy activities that may or may not feel refreshing to them. As a mom I rarely get a day off, certainly not once a week. If you work hard during the week, you may feel so tired that you just want to "veg out" on the weekend and not think about anything, let alone think about God. Being intentional is the last thing you want to do. But a big part of living in a Sabbath rhythm is deliberately choosing to do things that refresh you and bring you joy.

A generation ago almost all retail stores were closed Sunday. Even if you didn't attend church, there was a rhythm built into our culture of resting on Sundays. Work six days, rest for one. Now it's only the rare store that closes its doors on a day when many dual-income families do their shopping.

In certain parts of the country there are still "blue laws" on the books, which prevent the sale of certain things on Sundays. These laws (named for the blue paper on which the first ones were printed) originated with the Puritans in New England. They prohibit not only the sale of liquor but also theater shows, dancing, sports and other activities and businesses on Sundays. Most people see these as an old-fashioned inconvenience, not a reminder to rest.

In some states, including mine, car dealers are closed on Sundays. Certainly not known as a group for their moral uprightness or religious zeal, car dealers have figured out that being closed on Sunday is simply in their best interest. They've realized that they wouldn't sell more cars by being open on Sunday. They would just spread out their sales over seven days instead of six and have to cover the overhead costs of staying open an extra day. They understand it makes more sense to have a day off.

Like most of the rules God has given us, keeping the Sabbath is really in our best interest. We work better if we take an occasional day of rest. But I long for Sabbath rest, and not just because it's in my best interest. I know instinctively somehow that it will help my soul to flourish.

But how can I practice the Sabbath? As a mom I have responsibilities that preclude an entire day off. Many Sundays begin with church and a handful of good intentions, but busyness creeps in, unnoticed until we're lost in it. Home improvement projects, kids' social commitments, even cleaning up my office or doing a couple loads of laundry somehow steal the day. Even as I began to be more intentional about the Sabbath, it often seemed to get sabotaged. When I did manage to have a day of rest, it felt like it happened by accident.

Many of us carry a misconception that the Sabbath is a day of self-denial, a boring day governed by a list of things that are not allowed. While it is indeed a day to focus on God rather than ourselves, a prohibitive atmosphere misses the point. As I read and prayed about the Sabbath, I began to see that it was about making the day both joyful and restful.

In my search for help with keeping Sabbath, I read Carol Brazo's book *No Ordinary Home*, which chronicles her own struggles with this discipline. Like Carol, I longed for a way to make Sabbath special. The key, she eventually discovered, is preparation. She and her family begin getting ready for the Sabbath on Thursday. She cleans the house, prepares food ahead of time. Each week she and her husband reflect on a passage of Scripture that they discuss Saturday night after the children are in bed. Their main Sabbath meal is Saturday night, and Sunday's meals are mostly snacks and leftovers so she can have a rest from kitchen duty.

"To me it's essential that Sabbath never become a time of rules and restrictions," Brazo writes. "Some, including my dear Grandma Jo, might not appreciate my cross-stitching on the Sabbath. Cross-stitching is a luxury to me. A joy. If it feeds that part of us that creates, that celebrates beauty, it is allowed at our house. Sabbath is a time of wonder and healing."

I'd like to say that after reading this and other books on Sabbath, we began to practice it consistently in our house. We did begin it, but often times we let it slide. For a while we were reading stories from the children's Bibles after Sunday night dinner, but we haven't been consistent on that, either. But I haven't given up.

Incorporating any spiritual discipline into your life is not easy. The point is to keep trying. Pay attention to what God is drawing you to. If you try something and then let it slide for a year, don't despair. I have had to keep trying, and I've still got a long way to go. But I refuse to give up.

The Gift of the Sabbath

When I honor God with a Sabbath, I am finding that it is I who am blessed. When I give a day to God, he gives it back to me with a joyful reciprocity. God is honored; I am refreshed and rested. He makes good on his promise, "Those who honor me I will honor" (1 Samuel 2:30).

Getting to that result takes discipline and preparation. As a family we are still in process with this discipline. We are still figuring it out. Some Sundays are truly restful. Other Sundays we end up doing work that we should have done earlier in the week.

I'm learning that rather than focus on what I can't do, I focus on what I can do to help the fruit of the spirit flourish. What can I do to give and receive love? What brings me joy? How can I exercise self-control to create a peaceful and gentle day?

The Sabbath doesn't have to be on Sunday. If Scot has a busy schedule on the weekends, he'll take a day off during the week, and we'll schedule time together as a family for that day. If you have to work on Sunday, make another day your Sabbath, your restful, playful, prayerful day.

During the summer our day off is typically during the week. But the rest of the year I try to make Sunday a day of rest and play, at least for myself and the kids.

Sunday morning my focus is getting the kids out the door in time for church. But the rest of the day is blissfully unscheduled. Sometimes Scot has to work, but usually he can come to church with us and then head off to work after that. In spring and fall we have soccer games to attend, but I make sure that's our only obligation.

I leave the computer off on Sundays. I don't check my e-mail. I try to spend a lot of the day playing with the kids, reading, gardening or going for a walk.

In the previous chapter I described a Sunday morning

speaking gig. I don't do those anymore. Besides the fact that I don't want to work on Sunday, I also want to make the day a restful one for my family. My being gone on a Sunday morning makes my home just too chaotic.

We don't shop on Sundays and typically don't eat out, because both of those things would require someone else to work on Sunday. Okay, once in a while we'll order a pizza. We don't want to get too legalistic.

On Friday and Saturday I clean the house (some weeks better than others), so that I can enjoy resting in an uncluttered space. I don't prepare elaborate meals on Sunday, instead relying on snacks and leftovers, so that I have fewer kitchen responsibilities. But if the kids are keeping busy and don't need my attention, I might tackle a cooking project for the fun of it.

We dedicate the day to things that are fun or restful. The Sabbath should be a day of rest, but also of play. Not frantic, busy activity, but playful recreation that celebrates the good gifts that God has given us.

In summer we might go to a park or up to the lake to sail, if not on Sunday, then sometimes on Wednesday. Whatever day I choose, I try to be intentional about keeping it the Sabbath. I almost always spend a lot of time in the garden. While gardening may be considered work, it's something that I enjoy and it helps me to focus on God.

In fall we might watch football games on TV, or jump in the leaves, or go for a walk. In winter we might go sledding or simply cuddle in front of the fire. If Scot's working, the kids play in the basement or back yard (often with a friend or two), while I read a book or the Sunday *Chicago Tribune*, drinking coffee. Within the day I find time to simply sit, by the fireplace in winter, in the garden in summer, thanking God for his goodness.

Author Carol Brazo suggests starting Sabbath at sundown on Saturday and incorporating a family meal rich in ritual to Saturday night. A number of writers suggest meditating on a Scripture through the week that can then be discussed during a devotional time sometime during the Sabbath. I would love to do those things, but I'm still trying to figure out how. Now that we are beginning to create some space, I want to fill it up with God. I want corporate worship to be a part of the picture, rather than only my own private meditations. I want to become more intentional with my Sabbath, but I'm realizing you can't build traditions overnight.

Meanwhile, Sabbath has become a time of recreation that truly "re-creates" me, giving me and my family a fresh start and new energy for the week. We often include small traditions that build connection and joy for our family. We belong to a health club with an indoor pool, and many Sunday evenings we take the kids swimming. It's especially fun in winter, when there's something magical about the warm, humid, indoor pool. Standing in eighty-five-degree water and looking through the insulated windows at the snow feels like magic to my kids. Splashing around together is a way to connect as a family. We choose to do things that bring us joy.

We'll sometimes invite friends over for a meal on Sunday evenings. They have to be close enough friends that I don't have to feel that I need to impress them with how or what I serve. We can do pot-luck, or soup and sandwiches, or something simple we can throw on the grill.

What should you do or not do on the Sabbath? I can't tell you. I am learning that the Sabbath is not about rules. The Pharisees made up all kinds of nit-picky rules about dos and don'ts of the Sabbath, and Jesus rebuked them for it (Matthew 12:1-14).

The Sabbath is about, first of all, listening to God. It's a mindset of trust, a time for rest and reflection. What does "do not work" mean to you? What brings you joy? What can you do that is truly restful? It may mean something different to you than to me. Christian athletes sometimes have to work on Sunday. For that matter, so do pastors. They're doing their job from the pulpit every Sunday.

Perhaps for you another day of the week may be a better Sabbath. But don't just arbitrarily pick a day to be your Sabbath. Listen to God. He may call you, as he did Eric Liddell, to give up something to make Sunday special. He may not. The particular day is not as important as what you do with it. Again, the key is listening to what God is asking you to do.

As I've become more deliberate about the Sabbath, I've noticed some interesting things cropping up in the garden of my soul. I'm more peaceful, not just on Sundays, but through the week. I'm more disciplined with the housework on Saturday when I know that I'm preparing my home for a day of peace and rest. The discipline of slowing down on a daily basis becomes easier for me because I'm not just trying to slow down moment to moment. I'm looking at the rhythm of my week and trying to make the Sabbath the focus.

I have found that over time the Sabbath has become an easy yoke, a joyful gift that I give to God, to myself and to my family. By pruning our Sunday schedule we've allowed joy and peace and patience to grow in the garden of our souls.

 **Digging deeper**

1. What do your Sundays look like right now? What is your gut response to the idea of Sabbath? Why do you think God commanded us to take a day off?

2. List three steps you can take to begin practicing the Sabbath. Think about how you would create a restful, playful, prayerful day.

3. What activities re-create you? If someone told you to play, what would you do? What stands in the way of actually doing that very thing?

9

Harvest

Celebrating God's Gifts

The truth of a branch's life is found in the harvest.
The branch that remains in the Vine
will reap an abundance of fruit,
useful for the Master in extending his kingdom.
WAYNE JACOBSEN

*E*arly morning, late summer. I return from my walk before my family awakens. I pour myself a cup of coffee and wander out to the back yard, a rough wicker basket slung over my arm. I gather tomatoes, peppers and a bit of basil. I inspect the zucchini plants and discover a huge green squash under the leaves. It seems to have grown up overnight. I pick a cherry tomato and pop it into my mouth. It explodes with a taste of summer and sunshine. I set the hose to drip on the asters, which are nearly as tall as I am and getting ready to bloom. I pick some nasturtiums, trying to decide if I should arrange them in a tiny vase or use them to garnish a salad. I stop for a moment, the basket now heavy on my arm, and sip my coffee. Surrounded by the fruit of my garden, I am utterly delighted.

August and September are my favorite months in the garden. After planting and nurturing, hoeing and watering, killing slugs and pulling weeds, it is harvest time. I enjoy the process of gardening, watching as various flowers come into bloom, seeing seedlings grow taller and finally bearing fruit. The process is part of the fun. But the result, be it a bouquet of cutting flowers or a basket of tomatoes, is what makes the process worthwhile. It's the reason I cultivate a little piece of land.

My morning in the garden makes me wonder what delights

God. Why does God come into the garden of my soul? Why does he work the soil and pull the weeds and plant the seeds? What kind of harvest is he expecting?

Gardening—weeding, hoeing, working the soil and clearing out rocks—is hard work. And yet, when I get rid of weeds so that my flowers or tomatoes have room to wiggle their toes in the earth, it makes me smile. Despite the sweat and blisters I experience a certain sense of satisfaction working with the earth. The process itself is enjoyable.

I also love to see my garden making some kind of progress, which leads ultimately to a result: a harvest. Part of the reason I garden is to see things grow, and ultimately, for my plants to bloom or bear fruit. As wonderful as it is to see seedlings push through the earth each spring, what makes my joy complete is when I can sit down to eat a salad made entirely from things grown in my back yard, or when I can serve a friend coffee and a generous slice of zucchini bread made from that overgrown squash.

What would happen if I planted, weeded and tended my garden, but when the flowers bloomed or the vegetables ripened, I didn't pick any? What if I left the tomatoes on the vine for the chipmunks to eat, or let them fall off and rot on the ground, rather than enjoying them myself or sharing them with friends and family?

I'd enjoy the process, perhaps, but I'd miss the harvest. I'd miss one of the most wonderful things about gardening.

In the garden of my soul I often find myself working so hard that I overlook the harvest. I forget to notice the fruit that is being borne. I think I am sometimes afraid that it is somehow prideful to acknowledge, even to myself, the progress I am making on my spiritual journey. But I'm learning that if I want to cultivate my spiritual life, I need to celebrate the harvest and notice what the Master Gardener has done: how he's helped me grow, how he's blessed me, how he's been present with me in the midst of difficulties. Pride won't take root if I can remember that it is God's work in me that accounts for any growth or progress I may make.

Beyond that, I keep coming back to that question I asked myself that morning in the garden: What kind of a harvest is God looking for? When I say God is working in my life, what is he working *toward*?

Ultimately God is working in my life to make me a worshiper. Not just someone who sings hymns or praise choruses, but someone whose life continually glorifies God. Just as it is in the garden, being a worshiper is both a process and a result. We garden for both, and God does too. If we're somehow growing, pushing toward God like a seedling reaching for the sun, that's a kind of worship. Living a life that glorifies God, being a worshiper, looks different in each person's life and in different seasons of each life. Our church traditions, our personalities, our spiritual gifts and passions and temperaments, will all help define for each of us what it means to be a worshiper. No two gardens look exactly alike.

As I have thought about this question of why God would cultivate the garden of my soul, it raised even more questions. How do I become a worshiper? Duty or obligation may plant a few seeds, but they are unlikely to flourish. What was I hoping to achieve by inviting God into the garden of my soul? What's in it for him? What does a worshiper do?

How Can I Glorify God?
In my younger days I knew I was supposed to glorify God.

And I was on a pretty good track with this, as I knew a key part of glorifying God is being godly, that is, to act like Jesus would. It also had something to do with prayer and going to church. Unfortunately I thought that being godly involved a lot of rules and a lot of Boy Scout-style good deeds. I thought it meant being really serious and focused. It simply didn't occur to me that being godly meant being joyful.

"Joy is God's basic character," writes John Ortberg. "Joy is his eternal destiny. God is the happiest being in the universe."

Much of our joylessness (and it is, unfortunately, rampant among Christians) stems from not living in the moment, instead worrying about the past or the future. I remember hearing John give a message on this theme. At one point he said, "How much of your life do you spend waiting to live?" The question hit me like a truck. If I were to answer truthfully, I spent most of my life waiting to live. I had trouble enjoying the present moment, no matter what I was doing: working, spending time with my family. There were scattered moments, of course, where I found myself fully present and able to let go of worries about the past or future. But not many.

John talked about God's joyfulness in much the same words he uses in his book *The Life You've Always Wanted*. Then he said, "I give you permission to relentlessly pursue joy."

That message changed my life. I remember it even these many years later because I took notes on a scrap of paper and taped it to my bedroom mirror. "How much of your life do you spend waiting to live?" the paper asked me each morning. "Relentlessly pursue joy."

Not long after, I began taking some small steps, putting aside small windows of time to do some things that filled me up, that brought me joy.

When I stopped waiting for things to get better and just started doing things that made me feel joyful, amazingly I became more joyful, in spite of my circumstances. That "permission" from a spiritual mentor allowed me to do something I never thought possible. Pursuing joy opened doors that I continue to marvel at as I walk through them.

Pursuing joy in my vocation and in my own spiritual journey has transformed my life. I have found that it is really true that "the joy of the Lord is my strength." Pursuing joy has reintroduced me to the miracle of spiritual disciplines, which in turn have created more joy and a cause for celebration in my life. The joy comes from seeing what God is cultivating in the garden of my soul.

What's in It for God?

As I pondered the mystery of God, creator of the universe, gardening the soil of my soul, I kept asking, What's in it for God? Why does he persist in trying to cultivate this heart of joy and worship in me?

One of the most amazing things about God is that when his children worship him, he is utterly delighted. Our worship is his harvest. He is blessed by our worship. It brings him joy. The Bible says that when we give him praise and honor and glory with our words and with our lives, it's like a sweet-smelling offering, like an armload of fragrant flowers. He is blessed when we say, "You are worthy of our praise. You are worth living my life for."

Your worshipful response to God is the reason he

desires to cultivate the garden of your soul. Sometimes worship means just sitting in the garden, admiring the beauty of God. Do you think of him as beautiful? As the most wonderful being in the universe? When we say or sing, "Worthy is the Lamb," do we really believe it?

Until I truly believe that Jesus is *my* Lord because he's *the* Lord, the King of the Universe, I am not going to be free to worship him fully. Part of what he's trying to cultivate in my life is an ever-deepening understanding of who and what he is. When I catch glimpses of his beauty, of his brilliance, his unlimited wisdom and power, his deep loving concern for everything in his creation, worship is my only logical response. Like a sunflower turning its face toward the sun, I cannot do otherwise when his true light is revealed to me.

What is even more inspiring to me and almost incomprehensible is that Jesus, this utterly brilliant and powerful person, desires to walk in the garden with me. He is blessed by my worship, and not only because he knows it will help the fruit of the Spirit to grow abundantly in my life. He's just blessed by it, the way you are blessed when someone praises you, when your child tells you she loves you, when a friend expresses love and appreciation.

He desires our love in much the same way that we, his image bearers, desire his love. When we worship him, with songs or words or deeds, he doesn't just say, "Okay, you get a check mark on the chart today. You've fulfilled your obligations." Instead he says, "Wow, that's great! I'm so pleased. You bring me joy. Thank you."

God could have chosen to remain distant from us. He's all-powerful; he could have set up this world without the added complications that intimacy with his creatures involves. Or he could have created us in such a way that we'd have no choice but to worship him. But he didn't.

Instead, the Gardener of your soul gave you a choice. You can choose to enter into relationship with him. You can love him or you can refuse to. You can choose to let him cultivate the garden of your soul, or you can lock up the gate to the garden and keep him out. By giving us this choice, God also made a choice. He chose to risk that we would not choose him.

While God's self-esteem certainly does not hinge on my choices, he does care deeply about the choices I make. He longs for relationship, not out of any kind of neediness, but out of pure love. For that to be true God needs to allow us an intimate kind of access to himself. We can "approach the throne of grace with confidence" (Hebrews 4:16).

In a strange and mysterious way God chooses to make himself vulnerable. He chooses to suffer the pain of rejection. He also chooses to be able to feel the joy of intimacy with us.

If you don't believe this, look to the incarnation. By becoming one of us, he made himself extremely vulnerable, suffered pain and rejection, and also entered into deep friendship with human beings.

Whether we accept or reject him, God remains all-powerful and self-sufficient. The Bible says the whole creation, the whole universe, praises him (Psalm 19:1). If we didn't worship him, Jesus said, the rocks and stones would do it for us (Luke 19:40). God doesn't *need* us to worship him.

Yet, he seeks us out persistently. He chooses to pursue relationship, diligently and humbly working the garden of my soul in hopes of creating something beautiful, not necessarily just for my sake, but also for his. We are his image bearers, and he'd rather have praise from his children than from rocks. We have the ability, by inviting him into our lives and learning from him how to be a worshiper, to delight his heart.

What an incredible privilege! We can delight the heart of God, and we don't have to do it with our own power. We simply have to invite him in, allow him the kind of access that he is offering to us in return, and enjoy him.

The Westminster Catechism says that the chief end of man is to "glorify God and enjoy him forever." I want to glorify God in everything, not as a dreary obligation, but because I really enjoy him. But sometimes I don't glorify him. Sometimes when I get bogged down in life's details, I get angry and yell at my husband or my kids. Or just when I feel like I'm doing really well, I get blind-sided by conflict with, or criticism from, people who I think love me too little. I get overwhelmed with the details of motherhood and work and trying to juggle too many things, and I focus on my difficulties instead of on God. I forget to take time for joy, to worship him, to celebrate what he has done in my life.

What's amazing is that even then, God pursues relationship with me. Because of this, in spite of my shortcomings, I want to learn how to be a worshiper.

What Does a Worshiper Look Like?

A worshiper does more than just praise God by singing, although that is part of it. Worship is a spiritual discipline, but it is not just reserved for Sunday morning at church. God is working in the garden of my soul to grow me into someone that praises him with every aspect of my life. Frankly, he's got his work cut out for him!

In Romans 12 the apostle Paul says we are to offer our bodies as "living sacrifices, holy and pleasing to God—this is

your spiritual act of worship." What we do with our bodies—
with our work, our speech, our gifts, our actions—are ways
that we worship. Paul goes on to say that we should be transformed. Our willingness to let God change us is part of worship. How willing are you to let God change you?

When we submit to God's plowing through the hardened soil
of our souls, that's worship. Transformation, Paul writes, will help
us to see things from God's perspective, to be able to know God's
will (Romans 12:2), and to begin to act upon it. But transformation is a slow and round-about process, which, at least in my
experience, sometimes seems to go more backward than forward.

Transformation begins when we listen carefully to God,
allowing him intimate access to our souls. If we listen, we will
hear his call to love and serve others. In Romans 12 Paul also
talks about spiritual gifts. When we worship God by serving
him and others with our spiritual gifts, we are fulfilling our purpose. We're obeying what Jesus says is the greatest commandment: to love God and love our neighbor. In so doing we are
transformed, and the fruit of the Spirit can't help but grow.
That's the reason God is working in our lives. That's the harvest
he's hoping for.

In another passage about spiritual gifts, Ephesians 4, Paul
exhorts us to unity and to use our gifts to serve the body of
Christ "until we all reach unity in the faith and in the knowledge of the Son of God and become mature, attaining to the
whole measure of the fullness of Christ. Then we will no longer
be infants, tossed back and forth by the waves. . . . Instead,
speaking the truth in love, we will in all things grow up into him
who is the Head, that is, Christ" (vv. 13-15). God's aim for us,
his goal in working in our lives, is to move us toward maturity.
In our maturity we will not just offer God the praise of our

mouths, but also love him with our lives.

Ultimately worship is about love. First, love for God, but then, as Jesus commanded, for our neighbor. If the love of God transforms us, we cannot do other than to share that love with others, both by proclaiming God and serving his people.

"Yet a time is coming and has now come when the true worshipers will worship the Father in spirit and truth, for they are the kind of worshipers the Father seeks. God is spirit, and his worshipers must worship in spirit and in truth" (John 4:23-24).

The Father seeks. There's God, doing the seeking again, expecting a harvest of worship from his children. Take time to worship God, both privately and in community. Spend time just reading and meditating on the Psalms, which give us words to say that simply give God praise. The Bible calls us to worship him with our actions and to praise him with our mouths: "Praise the LORD. How good it is to sing praises to our God, how pleasant and fitting to praise him!" (Psalm 147:1). Singing God's praises, even if we are weary or don't feel like doing it, can transform our hearts. Still, God's goal is not to force us to praise him, but to create a heart in us that is so in love with him that worship is the only logical response.

In worship we see the truth about God and proclaim it. We bless God and he blesses us back. Marjorie Thompson notes, "Christian worship is paradoxical. God is both the audience and the main actor. We too are both actors and audience."

In the book of Revelation, John shares a vision of angels and creatures singing honor and glory and praise to the Lamb, Christ: "Day and night they never stop saying: Holy, holy, holy is the Lord God Almighty, who was, and is, and is to come" (Revelation 4:8). This is our destiny, what God is ultimately trying to create in us: a heart that knows him so well that we would desire nothing except to praise him.

But worship is also a discipline. We are called to be worshipers even when we don't see the truth about God, when he seems to be turning a deaf ear to our requests or simply keeping his distance. We are called to worship whether we feel like it or not. That's why God commanded all those celebrations in the Old Testament. He knew if he did not call us to worship, we might not do it. We'd miss the chance to know him better and be transformed. Worshiping when we may not feel like it can grow our faith like nothing else.

At my church we sing a song called "I Will Worship You." It's about worship as a discipline, about giving God praise even if he doesn't do what we want or expect; even when we can't, from our human perspective, see what he's really up to. One line says, "I will worship you, when all hope seems gone, I will stand and proclaim that you are my God, yes, you are my God, I will worship you." Whether or not God answers our Santa Claus-letter prayers, whether or not he makes our lives easy or blesses our efforts doesn't change his worthiness. God is worthy of praise even when we are disappointed with what he does or does not do. We proclaim his power and his ownership of our lives no matter what.

We are to praise him, yet we can still be honest if we are frustrated or disappointed with him. Worship often means simple obedience. When I show up at church, even if I've had a tough day, and engage in worship, my heart is healed. When I'm willing to say out loud, together with a community of believers, how awesome God is, I know the truth of what we're saying and singing more clearly. The music and the words and the being with others in community have a mysterious power to heal and transform us.

A Command to Rejoice

"Rejoice in the Lord always. I will say it again: Rejoice!" Paul instructs us in Philippians 4:4. Throughout Scripture, God commands his people to rejoice. Why?

I used to think of the Old Testament as a book of interesting stories, but also of restrictive, obscure laws and some downright unusual battle stories. But much of God's law is about feasts and festivals, which instituted a regular rhythm of celebrations. Some were serious, some were more lighthearted. All of them were designed to commemorate the activity of God in the lives of his people. God commanded the Israelites to hold these celebrations each year, whether or not the people felt like celebrating. You'd think God wouldn't have to command his people to celebrate, but he did then and he still does today.

Biblical celebrations often involved commands to enjoy the best food and drink, commands to sing and tell stories, commands to dance and worship God. Deuteronomy 14 has specific instructions from God for celebrating the harvest each year, which included taking a tithe of the harvest, using it for rich food and strong drink and enjoying it in a joyful celebration. But the food and drink were not the focus: Worshiping God for his goodness was the focus of the celebration.

Celebration is a gift, but also a spiritual discipline. And like other disciplines, celebration has the power to transform our hearts. Some even argue that celebration is the most important of all spiritual disciplines. "Celebration is central to all the Spiritual Disciplines," writes Richard Foster. "Without a joyful spirit of festivity the Disciplines become dull, death-breathing tools in the hands of modern Pharisees. Every Discipline should be characterized by carefree gaiety and a sense of thanksgiving."

Living Jubilant Lives

Entire sections of the Old Testament are devoted to specific celebration instructions from God. Leviticus 23–25 records God's words to Moses about all of the feasts the children of Israel were to celebrate, beginning with a weekly Sabbath. The chapters also spell out instructions for Passover, the Feast of Weeks, the Feast of Trumpets, the Day of Atonement and the Feast of Tabernacles. Chapter 25 caps off the list with the most incredible commandment of celebration of all, the Year of Jubilee: "Consecrate the fiftieth year and proclaim liberty throughout the land to all its inhabitants. It shall be a jubilee for you; each one of you is to return to his family property and his own clan" (Leviticus 25:10).

In the Year of Jubilee debts were to be cancelled, slaves freed, land returned to its original owner. People who had worked as slaves came home to their families. Even commerce was affected by the prospect of the upcoming Jubilee. The price you could sell a piece of land for depended on how many years before the Jubilee year it was: the fewer years to go, the lower the price.

In the Year of Jubilee, like other Sabbath years, God's people were commanded to neither plant nor prune nor harvest. The people were to trust the grace and provision of God.

Unfortunately many Bible scholars believe that the Sabbath years for the land and the Year of Jubilee were rarely, if ever, celebrated. Some of these scholars even contend that the exile into Babylon was the consequence of ignoring God's law about observing the Year of Jubilee and the Sabbath for the land.

Why didn't God's people obey his directive for a Year of Jubilee? Well, it was a pretty radical commandment. If you had purchased land, would you be willing to give it back to its original owner after fifty years? If someone owed you money, would you forgive his debt just because it was the year for it? I don't know if I would.

A Jubilee commandment certainly flies in the face of our economic system, capitalism. It goes against every human instinct of self-preservation. It runs counter to our pull-yourself-up-by-the-bootstraps mentality. But it was not a capricious command. The Jubilee was a call to unfathomable trust in God's provision. It was a reminder that God owns everything, and his people are simply stewards of the land and all of God's gifts.

Think about the Jubilee from the perspective of a slave: someone who had sold his land and himself into slavery just to stay alive. The Jubilee would be an incredible gift: a second chance at life, a chance to start over.

The good news for us is that the Jubilee was not only a commandment, but a prophecy. Spiritually, the Bible says, we are in slavery. We are the poor in spirit, living in spiritual poverty. Despite our attempts at good works, we are morally bankrupt. We need a Jubilee. And we've been given it. We have been given grace and freedom, and our debt of sin has been cancelled. In the words of songwriter Michael Card, "Jesus is our Jubilee."

In Jesus we are set free; we are given God's favor. Through him God has provided for our deepest need. The Jubilee concept is a radical one. Yet the message of Jesus is the same, and just as radical. Through him we are redeemed from the slavery of sin, and we can come home to our family, his family. And because of that freedom through Christ, Richard Foster notes, "We are called into a perpetual Jubilee of the Spirit."

Yet, how often do we live jubilant lives? When someone says, "Hello, how are you?" we say, "Fine" or "Okay." Unless something wonderful has happened, we don't say, "Great!" and even if it has, we don't respond, "Jubilant!"

I'm not talking about pretending to be happy. God doesn't want plastic followers. He is calling us to a joy that transcends our circumstances because it is focused on him. We may shake our heads at the children of Israel, but are we that different from them? I have trouble trusting. How easily I take for granted the fact that Jesus has not only declared a Jubilee of Spirit, but that he is available to me, that he wants to joyfully tend the garden of my soul. But when I can catch a glimpse of the incredible gift that Jesus has given me, it makes me want to live a jubilant life: to let joy grow. I do not naturally do this, however, which is why I need the discipline of celebration.

In celebration we remember what God has done: celebrating communion, we remember the crucifixion; celebrating Christmas, we remember the incarnation.

God gives purpose to our partying. In our society partying is often associated with overindulgence or even drunkenness. It's what people do to forget how hard their life is: their stress at work, the struggles of their marriage, their disappointment.

Spiritual celebration, on the other hand, is not about forgetting, but about remembering. Remembering with joy how God has been faith-

185

ful. How he's given us strength to handle the stress at work, how he's assured us of his presence even as we struggle in our marriages or with a wayward child.

Celebration is not a denial of our difficulties or a way of escaping the pain of the trials we face. It's a recognition of God's presence in the midst of these struggles and a reminder of the good things he's done. Without it I would tend to remember only the trials and forget the small and wonderful ways God has been working in the garden of my soul.

As John Ortberg writes, "When we celebrate, we exercise our ability to see and feel goodness in the simplest gifts of God. We are able to take delight today in something we wouldn't even have noticed yesterday. Our capacity for joy increases."

Cultivating with Passion

There are gardens, and then there are *gardens*. When I look through garden books or magazines, or visit the homes of true gardeners, then compare it to my own back yard, I can only sigh. I have flowers, vegetables, trees and shrubs. Those other gardens do too. Yet they have something I haven't yet achieved, although I hope I'm moving in that direction. It's a beauty not just of individual plants, but of the whole, which is greater than the sum of its parts. There's cohesiveness in some gardens that draws you in and makes you want to stay there.

I think the most beautiful and luxurious gardens are those tended by passionate gardeners. A gardener who sees the garden as a canvas for personal expression, who celebrates the earth and what you can do with some seeds and dirt, is more likely to have one of those beautiful and amazing gardens. Passionate gardeners spend more than just a few hours on the weekends tending their gardens. For them, gardening is a daily discipline and a daily joy.

Celia Thaxter was a passionate gardener. She wrote:

> Often I hear people say, "How do you make your plants flourish like this?" as they admire the little flower patch I cultivate in summer, or the window gardens that bloom for me in the winter; "I can never make my plants blossom like this! What is your secret?" And I answer with one word, "Love." For that includes all—the patience that endures continual trial, the constancy that makes perseverance possible, the power of foregoing ease of mind and body to minister to the necessities of the thing beloved, and the subtle bond of sympathy which is as important, if not more so, than all the rest.

The discipline of celebration increases my passion. It is what transforms the garden of my soul from a bunch of varied plants into a beautiful cohesive garden. When I regularly celebrate, I begin to see the fruit of the Spirit growing in the garden of my soul: not just joy but also love and peace and patience, and everything else that a Spirit-filled life is about. Celebration invites the presence of the Spirit and brings all the aspects of Spirit-filled living together. It is a way of remembering that God is working in my life, and he's motivated by love. His love causes his children to flourish. In celebration I gain a proper perspective on the weeds and hard work because of the fruit God is producing in my life. Celebration increases my passion.

Dallas Willard writes, "Celebration heartily done makes our deprivations and sorrows seem small, and we find in it great strength to do the will of our God because his goodness becomes so real to us."

Even when trials and difficulties have been a part of your life, the Master Gardener can use them to grow your faithfulness and patience. We need to take time to see what God has done and to celebrate it.

Celebrating the Extra-Ordinary Moments

We tend to make a big deal of big events, but what about little ones? Celebration is a discipline, and we should engage in it on a daily basis. Certainly the fruit of joy will flourish if we daily ask ourselves: what can I celebrate today? I am not talking about a Pollyanna approach to life. I'm not asking you to pretend everything is fine when it's not. I'm talking about living with your eyes open, watching for what God is doing.

One way to make celebration a daily discipline is to look for brief moments of wonder in your day. Pay attention, notice what is going on around you. Look for something to thank God for, some small reason to worship him.

Often in the winter, late in January, the weather in Chicago thaws briefly. It will rain or sleet for a few days, turning the snow gray and washing much of it away. It is hard to find ways to celebrate. Everyone around me seems grumpy and we suffer from collective seasonal affective disorder.

So in January, if we get a few days when the temperatures rise slightly but the wind stays chilly, I venture into the back yard and trim a few branches from my forsythia bushes. Their buds are clenched tightly shut, but if I bring them inside, where it's a balmy sixty-nine degrees, and put them in a vase of water, they will bloom within a week or two. Fragile yellow blossoms and green leaves provide a stark but hopeful contrast against the snow that inevitably comes storming back in late February or March. The forsythia blooming on my windowsill are a reminder to pause, to celebrate, to be just a little more grateful, a little bit hopeful that spring really will come again.

Celebration is also about becoming playful, responding to what God gives in each moment with a child-like wonder. This playfulness, this wonder, does not come naturally to many grownups, myself included.

When my second child was just a baby, I remember trying to read a little book titled *When I Relax I Feel Guilty* by Tim Hansel. I could totally relate to the title. It could have been my life motto. But I scoffed at his antidote to the guilt: learn to play. "I don't have time to play," I said. A wise friend pointed out that I spent the vast majority of my time with two children under the age of two. Isn't play what children do?

This gentle rebuke led to a shattering revelation. I was not very good at simply playing just for the fun of it. Two kids just less than two years apart is work, no doubt. But it certainly has its playful potential as well. I needed to learn how to do something that had no ulterior motive, no long-term purpose other than having fun.

I had been a mom for two years, and while I did play with my daughter, I was always thinking about how to stimulate her neurons or build her vocabulary more than I ever thought about simply having fun. I wanted her to have fun, I guess, but I never even thought about that as a goal for myself.

I lived intensely, even in my recreation: sailing, tennis, weightlifting. My approach to these activities was purposeful, not playful. I was out to win, to get in shape, to achieve something. Play, ironically, was not a part of it.

Today, several years later, I am still an intense person. I always will be I think. But I am learning how to play, how to dress up and dance around the family room with my kids, or stage mock weddings, balls or Disney video re-enactments ("Mom, I'll be Pocahontas, Aaron will be John Smith and you can be Meeko the raccoon," my daughter tells me. It's hard to take yourself too seriously if you are cast as a raccoon.) I'm learning how to play tennis just for the fun of it, how to not beat myself up every time I miss a shot. I am learning to accept myself, to be playful, to lighten up for heaven's sake—literally. I am learning that playfulness, child-like joy, is not a sign of laziness or weakness. It allows God to strengthen us.

"Celebration brings joy into life, and joy makes us strong," writes Foster. "Often I am inclined to think that joy is the motor, the thing that keeps everything else going. Without joyous celebration to infuse the other Disciplines, we will sooner or later abandon them. Joy produces energy. Joy makes us strong."

When I pursue joy, when I take the time to notice things— the first snow of winter, the first flower of spring, the way God is cultivating patience and peace in my life—I discover God, who, as I said before, is the most joyful being in the universe. I also get better at accepting myself, and I am more aware of God's unconditional acceptance of me. As a bonus I am better equipped to love and accept others as a result.

What Makes You Feel Closest to God?

Before we can engage in authentic worship and celebration, we need to examine our relationship with God. We need to examine our own hearts. What makes you feel closest

to God? What brings you joy? Is it when he does what you want him to, answering your prayers the way you want him to? Although that may seem like a logical answer, the reverse is actually true: you will experience joy when you do what God wants you to.

"Joy comes through obedience to Christ and joy results from obedience to Christ. Without obedience joy is hollow and artificial," Foster notes. Obedience begins when we open the garden gate and invite Christ in. By allowing him his rightful place, we have taken the first step of obedience.

In order to engage in the disciplines of celebration and worship, we must circle back to where we began, with self-examination. What work needs to be done? What seeds need to be planted? My garden is not likely to do well if I plant cacti or palm trees, since I live in the Midwest. I need to know what will thrive here.

Likewise, I need to know myself if I am to engage in meaningful celebration. I need to look at what God has done, how he has created me, the passions and loves and gifts he has given me. To live in a way that reflects my uniqueness is actually a way of obediently worshipping God.

My husband, for example, loves tennis and sailing. These things bring him joy, especially because he works a lot and doesn't always have time for them. When he takes time for these things, he needn't feel guilty. These things re-create him; they refresh and replenish his soul. They are spiritual activities, and he is, in a way, obeying God by engaging in them. As an added bonus, sailing and tennis are also recreation that Scot and I can enjoy together. By enjoying them together, we reconnect, strengthening the bond between us.

All of life can be spiritual. If you really love going for walks or doing crafts or going camping, you don't need to feel like those things are not spiritual. I happen to feel very close to God when I am downhill skiing. Being on a mountain somehow increases my proximity to heaven, and not just because of the elevation.

It's that I just love to ski. I'm not an excellent skier, but I enjoy it, just for the love of it. I love looking at the mountains, feeling the wind in my face, the exhilaration of a challenging hill.

For our tenth anniversary Scot and I skied in Banff, Canada, which in my book is one of the most beautiful places in North America. "This is what heaven looks like," I told Scot as we stood at the top of the mountain, the Canadian Rockies rising majestically around us, fresh powder inviting us down the run in front of us. "And this is what you get to do there."

Because I live in the Midwest, I don't get a chance to do a lot of great skiing very often. I can't rely on mountain-top experiences for joy, figuratively or literally, so I strive to look for more ordinary moments to celebrate, to experience joy.

The Gift of the Vine

In mid-July I noticed a vine growing in my perennial bed. At first I thought it to be a weed, but upon closer examination of its huge lobed leaves and spiny stem, I realized it was some kind of squash. I was perplexed as to how it got into the flower bed, since I hadn't planted squash anywhere near that side of the yard.

I'd better pull that up, I thought. But since I spent most of this summer writing about gardening my soul instead of actually gardening in my yard, I didn't get to it right away. Truth be told, I was a little frustrated at how little gardening I'd had a chance to do this summer.

Then one day, strengthened by my neglect, the vine bloomed. I was making coffee and looked out through the kitchen window at my garden. A single bright yellow-orange star-shaped flower bigger than my hand greeted the morning. It was so lovely that I decided to let the squash vine stay. By the end of the day the bloom had faded, but the next day another bloom was there, the first thing I saw when I stood at the sink making breakfast.

How did the vine get there? I didn't plant it. Perhaps an animal had buried the seed or dropped it there. The kids and I spun stories about the squirrels planting squash, and I began to look forward to seeing those arrestingly beautiful blooms. I wondered why God makes so many flowers in the shape of stars. One day I noticed the start of a bit of fruit on the vine. It looked like it might be zucchini. I looked through garden books trying to identify exactly what it was, but I couldn't tell. I let it keep growing.

Since I didn't know what it was, I started calling the vine the Morning Star, because it bloomed stars each morning. Then I remembered that Jesus calls himself "the bright Morning Star" (Revelation 22:16) and also the "true vine" (John 15:1). The vine gave me a daily glimpse of God's grace: a free gift of beauty and mystery, new every morning.

I didn't plant the vine, but most mornings its bright yellow stars greeted me. It brought beauty to my yard in a season when I was too busy writing to give my garden the attention it really needed. The vine reminded me of everything I've been learning as I write this book: Given the right conditions for growth, who knows what God will plant and grow?

Eventually the little fruit on the vine took on a spherical shape, so I thought it might be one of those new gourmet types of round zucchini, or perhaps some kind of melon. I thought about picking it, but the stem looked too thick. Squash usually slip off the vine when they are ripe. So I waited. The Morning Star vine was teaching me patience.

In the last week of August the round squash began to show

speckles of orange through its skin. The stem got thicker. The ribs along the side of the fruit grew more pronounced. I realized that our vine had grown a pumpkin! The kids were delighted. It's still on the vine, although the vine is starting to whither and it doesn't flower anymore. It's a rather petite pumpkin, but now bright orange, brightening up the corner of the flower bed. The kids are talking about the possibility of pumpkin pie or a mini jack-o'-lantern. Every day I can't help but notice the pumpkin that God sent me: a picture of his provision and grace, which grew without my planting or help; a lesson in patience; a teaching tool on enjoying the process as much as the end result.

A Beautiful and Amazing Garden

I am realizing that my little Morning Star vine, the providential pumpkin, has provided some answers to the question I posed at the beginning of this book: How can I live in such a way that the fruit of the Spirit grows in my life?

While certain practices, which we've discussed in this book, can help us to answer that question, we each approach spiritual growth in different ways. The garden of your soul is somewhat like mine, but it also reflects your uniqueness. This is not to say you can create your own spirituality. It just means you need to pay attention to what God is doing in your life, what he's calling you to, how he created you.

During the many years I have been a Christian, I have had seasons of growth. God has planted his Word, through the Bible or godly teachers, and I've been amazed by his work in my life. But I've also had seasons where God didn't seem to plant much. If I read my Bible (which I did infrequently), I did so out of obligation, sort of mindlessly, without really thinking about why I was doing it or what I thought would be the result. Or I'd work really hard at "religious" tasks, but end up nowhere. During those seasons not much fruit grew in the garden of my soul. I was frustrated, disappointed and unsure of how to get things growing again. Sometimes I didn't even care about my spiritual life and just let the garden of my soul get choked with weeds and thistles.

Looking back, one of my problems was that I didn't realize that my soul is a garden and that it has seasons of planting, seasons of harvest, seasons of growth and seasons of rest. I also mistakenly thought I was entirely in charge of my own growth. But I'm learning that God is the one who's working in me. I can help create the right conditions for growth, but ultimately I can't do it myself. That's not to say I should sit back and expect God to do everything. I need to cooperate with him.

For me, gardening is not just a picture or an analogy for my spiritual life. It's an integral part of my spiritual life. I meet God many places, but mostly I meet him outdoors. To me, it is no coincidence that gardening is done on our knees.

Being outside, whether I'm gardening, skiing or enjoying the solitude of the woods, fills me up. It waters my soul. Love, joy, peace and patience all come to me when I have intimate contact with creation, when there is dirt under my nails or snow in my face.

But right now I'm at the computer. The dryer is buzzing, my kids are downstairs yelling, "Hey Mommmm!" and the deadline for this book is looming. I'm thinking of phone calls I should make and what to

microwave for dinner. I'm wishing I could go sit in the garden instead of writing about gardening.

Whether I am writing, gardening or trying to spend time in prayer, there are always other tasks and people (worthy as they may be) that would pull me away from any of these life-giving activities. Maybe this happens to you. I have a feeling I'm not the only one who gets distracted.

In the midst of the chaos and distractions you can invite the Master Gardener into the garden of your soul. Let him plant the seeds of truth, pull up the weeds of doubt and sin. Then expect a harvest. When I plant cucumbers, I don't expect geraniums. Nor do I expect the cucumbers to be withered and tasteless. Instead, I look for cucumber seedlings and nurture them. I stake them so the vines can grow, I protect them from beetles with row covers. I water and fertilize and weed. Later in summer I buy vinegar and salt and get the canning jars ready for making pickles. I expect a harvest. However, I don't expect it the day after I plant the seeds. I expect it in due season. God's promises of fruitfulness don't include instant gratification. Psalm 1 says that a person who is blessed is like a tree planted by a stream, which "yields its fruit in season." I need to expect a harvest, but wait patiently for it.

Despite the weeds and rocks I believe that God wants to till the garden of my soul. His vision for my life is not just a few straggly plants and wilted flowers. Nor is it row upon row of cabbages and potatoes, although nourishing things are likely to have their place. He is a passionate gardener who is working to make the garden of my soul a place of both beauty and productivity, where the fruit of the Spirit flourishes. I want to work with him, to be as intentional with my spiritual life as I am with my cucumbers.

He's aiming to grow me into someone who loves him, worships him and loves other people, even the ones who don't love me. For that matter, to love even the ones who do love me, but still aggravate me.

He's helping me to see that joy is indeed strength, and he's cultivating a desire in me for his joy.

He's calling me to keep the garden fence in good repair so that I can have times of solitude where I will experience his peace and then be able to carry that peace with me into times of difficulty.

He's patiently working the soil, improving it. He's teaching me, through my real garden and my real life, with pumpkin vines and preschoolers, the value of patiently waiting on him. He's pulling weeds of impatience and hurry.

As love, joy, peace and patience grow, he's planting seeds of kindness all over my life, and I find myself wanting to be as kind to others as he has been to me.

He's given me so many good things: people, provisions, possessions. The more I see that goodness, the more I want to slow my life down so that I can appreciate it and have time to share it with others.

He keeps showing me his faithfulness, and he's cultivating in me a desire for the habits of faithfulness, like prayer and Sabbath-keeping.

He's introducing me to a more gentle way of approaching my spiritual life. He's been watering the garden with a gentle rain, rather than a flood, patiently teaching me to be gentler in my approach to everything from reading Scripture to caring for my family.

He's been carefully and methodically taking over control of the garden because I've slowly been letting him. I've been learning about self-control, which is really controlling my *self*, keeping my ego from trying to run the show. He's been teaching me to say no to certain things so that I can say yes to him. He's been showing me that self-control is really God-control.

Like my backyard garden, the garden of my soul still has to be weeded regularly and protected from marauding pests. I sometimes neglect it or lock up the gate and forget to invite the Master Gardener in. It has dry seasons. Winter comes on a regular basis. The soil gets depleted and needs rest. Sometimes it seems that growth takes a long time.

Such is the nature of gardens . . . and souls. Yet, I am not discouraged. I know that the garden of my soul is tended by a passionate gardener. As the seasons unfold, it will become a place that reflects his skillful and loving cultivation, a place where love, joy, peace, patience, kindness, goodness, faithfulness, gentleness and self-control are flourishing. He's working joyfully there to grow a heart of worship . . . a life that glorifies him . . . a beautiful and amazing garden.

Digging deeper

1. When you think of worshiping God, what comes to mind? How do you think you could worship God with your actions?

2. God calls us to celebrate, to live jubilant lives. What gets in the way of your having a jubilant spirit? What are some things God has done lately that you could celebrate?

3. Marjorie Thompson writes that spiritual disciplines are like garden tools. Of the disciplines we've discussed in this book, which one is your soul's garden most in need of these days? What can you do to incorporate that discipline into your life?

Notes

Chapter 1: Winter

The opening quote is from Mirabel Osler in *A Gentle Plea for Chaos: Reflections from an English Garden* (London: Bloomsbury, 1989), p. 7.

Eugene Peterson's rendering of John 15:10 is from his Bible translation *The Message* (Colorado Springs: NavPress, 1993), p. 260.

John Ortberg's words on spiritual transformation are from *The Life You've Always Wanted* (Grand Rapids, Mich.: Zondervan, 1997), p. 197. John also introduced me to the idea of *training* rather than *trying* to grow spiritually.

Chapter 2: Soil

The epigraph is from Vigen Guroian's *Inheriting Paradise: Meditations on Gardening* (Grand Rapids, Mich.: Eerdmans, 1999), p. 5.

Henry Cloud's comments on Luke 13 are from *Changes That Heal* (Grand Rapids, Mich.: Zondervan, 1990), p. 30.

The thoughts on spiritual disciplines are from Marjorie Thompson's *Soul Feast* (Louisville, Ky.: Westminster John Knox, 1995), p. 10.

Thompson's quote on self-examination is again from *Soul Feast*, p. 83. Her chapter on this topic provides excellent and practical details on both life review and daily examen disciplines.

The quote by Dallas Willard is from *The Spirit of the Disciplines* (San Francisco: Harper & Row, 1988), p. 138.

Chapter 3: Fence

The epigraph is from the preface of Lois Trigg Chaplin's *A Garden's Blessings* (Minneapolis: Augsburg, 1993).

"The garden fence . . ." My thoughts on solitude have been shaped by many authors and teachers, and by my own experience of it. While the garden fence word picture is mine, it was one of my spiritual mentors, Ruth H. Barton, who pointed out that solitude is, as she put it, "a container for all the other disciplines."

Vigen Guroian's thoughts on garden as retreat are from the preface of his collection of essays, *Inheriting Paradise: Meditations on Gardening* (Grand Rapids, Mich.: Eerdmans, 1999).

Hearing God is by Dallas Willard (Downers Grove, Ill.: InterVarsity Press, 1984), pp. 18, 56.

Marjorie Thompson's thoughts on contemplative prayer are from *Soul Feast* (Louisville, Ky.: Westminster John Knox, 1995), p. 45.

The quote from Dietrich Bonhoeffer is from *Life Together* (San Francisco: HarperCollins, 1954), pp. 77-78.

Jill Murphy's book *Five Minutes Peace* was published in 1986 by Putnam.

Chapter 4: Mess

The epigraph by Rudyard Kipling is quoted in *Wisdom from the Garden*, comp. and ed. Criswell Freeman (Nashville, Tenn.: Delaney Street Press, 2000), p. 52.

Gilbert Bilezikian's thoughts on community are from *Community 101* (Grand Rapids, Mich.: Zondervan, 1997), pp. 43-44.

Parker Palmer's words are from *Let Your Life Speak* (San Francisco: Jossey-Bass, 2000), p. 103.

The quote by Dietrich Bonhoeffer is from *Life Together* (San Francisco: HarperCollins, 1954), p. 19.

Henri Nouwen's insights on community are from an article titled "From Solitude to Community to Ministry," *Leadership Journal*, Spring 1995.

Parker Palmer's quote about community is from *Let Your Life Speak*, p. 92.

Judith Couchman's thoughts on knowing our purpose are from *Designing a Woman's Life* (Sisters, Ore.: Multnomah Press, 1995), p. 41.

The passage by John Ortberg is from *The Life You've Always Wanted* (Grand Rapids, Mich.: Zondervan, 1997), p. 162. Even where not directly quoted, John Ortberg's insights on the discipline of secrecy, from his teaching at Willow Creek Community Church and as written in *The Life You've Always Wanted*, have been enormously helpful.

Douglas Steere is quoted in Marjorie Thompson's *Soul Feast* (Louisville, Ky.: Westminster John Knox, 1995), p. 37.

Chapter 5: Seed

The epigraph is from Celia Thaxter, an extraordinary gardener and writer, as evidenced by the longevity of her book *An Island Garden* (1894; reprint, Boston: Houghton Mifflin, 1988), p. 25.

"Asking ourselves, 'What would Jesus do?'" is from Dallas Willard, *The Spirit of the Disciplines* (San Francisco: Harper & Row, 1988), p. 9.

Bruce Wilkinson's popular book is *The Prayer of Jabez* (Sisters, Ore.: Multnomah Press, 2000).

Mirabel Osler's quote on a garden's soul is from *A Gentle Plea for Chaos: Reflections from an English Garden* (London: Bloomsbury, 1989), p. 16.

Joyce Sackett's thoughts are from *In God's Garden* (Wheaton, Ill.: Tyndale House, 1998), p. 10.

Henri Nouwen's insights on patience are from the reading for January 5 in his daybook *Bread for the Journey* (San Francisco: HarperSanFrancisco, 1997).

Chapter 6: Water

"The cliff of safety . . ." is from Larry Crabb's book *The Marriage*

Builder (Grand Rapids, Mich.: Zondervan, 1982), p. 40.

Richard Foster's thoughts on reading Scripture are from *Celebration of Discipline* (San Francisco: Harper & Row, 1988), p. 29.

The quotation from John Ortberg comes from *The Life You've Always Wanted* (Grand Rapids, Mich.: Zondervan, 1997), pp. 185-86.

Frederick Buechner's words come from *Whistling in the Dark: A Doubter's Dictionary* (San Francisco: HarperCollins, 1993).

Eugene Peterson's rendering of Ephesians 2 is from *The Message* (Colorado Springs: NavPress, 1993), p. 476.

Sydney Eddison's thoughts on gardening notebooks are from *The Self-Taught Gardener* (New York: Viking, 1997), pp. 13, 142, 143.

Madeleine L'Engle's thoughts on prayer are from *Walking on Water: Reflections on Faith and Art* (New York: Bantam, 1982), p. 96.

Marjorie Thompson's insights on prayer are from *Soul Feast* (Louisville, Ky.: Westminster John Knox, 1995), p. 31.

Kathleen Norris's quote is from *Amazing Grace: A Vocabulary of Faith* (New York: Riverhead, 1998).

For helpful information on the topic of latter rains, read the *New Bible Commentary*, ed. D. Guthrie and J. A. Motyer (Grand Rapids, Mich.: Eerdmans, 1970), especially the notes on Joel 2:23. Also, I'd like to thank Jan Frank for her wise instruction on this topic.

The quote from Marjorie Thompson in question one of "Digging Deeper" is from *Soul Feast*, p. 19.

Chapter 7: Space

Ken Gire's quote is from *The Reflective Life* (Colorado Springs: Chariot Victor, 1998), p. 43.

Wayne Jacobsen writes about spiritual truth learned in a vineyard in *In My Father's Vineyard* (Dallas: Word, 1997), p. 105.

Marjorie Thompson's comments are from *Soul Feast* (Louisville, Ky.: Westminster John Knox, 1995), p. 71.

The quote by Elisabeth Elliot is from her book *Discipline: The Glad*

Surrender (Old Tappan, N.J.: Revell, 1982), p. 46.

Marjorie Thompson's thoughts on fasting are again from *Soul Feast*, p. 71.

The quote beginning "A friend of mine . . ." is from Elisabeth Elliot's *Discipline: The Glad Surrender*, p. 48.

Chapter 8: Rest

The epigraph by Katrina Kenison is from *Mitten Strings for God* (New York: Warner Books, 2000), p. 179. Her chapter on Sabbath is lovely.

Carol Brazo's words are from *No Ordinary Home* (Sisters, Ore.: Multnomah Press, 1995), p. 60. The entire chapter on Sabbath is very practical and helpful.

Although I do not quote from it, Dorothy C. Bass has written a great book on slowing and Sabbath titled *Receiving the Day: Christian Practices for Opening the Gift of Time* (San Francisco: Jossey-Bass, 2000). I heartily recommend reading it.

Chapter 9: Harvest

Wayne Jacobsen's epigraph is from *In My Father's Vineyard* (Dallas: Word, 1997), p. 79.

John Ortberg's insights on joy are quoted from *The Life You've Always Wanted* (Grand Rapids, Mich.: Zondervan, 1997), p. 67.

"God chooses to make himself vulnerable . . ." Note: my deepest thanks to my pastor John Ortberg for helping me clarify my thinking on these points.

Marjorie Thompson's quote about Christian worship is from *Soul Feast* (Louisville, Ky.: Westminster John Knox, 1995), p. 45.

The song "I Will Worship You" was written by Joe Horness and Curt Coffield, © Ever Devoted Music, 2001. Used with permission.

Richard Foster's quote is from *Celebration of Discipline* (San Francisco: Harper & Row, 1988), p. 191.

My comments on the Jubilee and Sabbath commandments being ignored are based on conversations with several scholars and also on reading the *New Bible Commentary,* ed. D. Guthrie and J. A. Motyer (Grand Rapids, Mich.: Eerdmans, 1970), especially the notes on Leviticus 26:34-39 and 2 Chronicles 36:21.

Richard Foster's quote about the perpetual Jubilee of the Spirit is from *Celebration of Discipline,* p. 190.

John Ortberg's words are from his *Life You've Always Wanted,* p. 72.

Celia Thaxter's thoughts on gardening are from *An Island Garden* (1894; reprint, Boston: Houghton Mifflin, 1988), pp. 4ff.

The quote by Dallas Willard is from *The Spirit of the Disciplines* (San Francisco: Harper & Row, 1988), p. 181.

Tim Hansel's book *When I Relax I Feel Guilty* was published in 1979 by David C. Cook.

Richard Foster's insights on joy are from *Celebration of Discipline,* the first quote from p. 191, the latter one from p. 192.